Verbatimly, Trump

The Mockiography™ Branded Political Satire About President Trump

Vol. 1: Steady State Of Confusion

By Anonymous and Cam Stanton Meyer VII

WANTED

PRESIDENT TRUMPY'S <u>BRAIN</u> HAS GONE ROGUE AND IS NOW MISSING!! ALL THAT IS KNOWN IS... THE CHINESE GOVERNMENT THINKS IT'S <u>VERY, VERY LARGE</u>, BUT EVERYONE ELSE THINKS IT'S <u>VERY, VERY *TINY*</u> *(That's what she said! <u>Seriously!</u>)*. ANY SIGHTINGS MUST BE REPORTED IMMEDIATELY TO YOUR LOCAL <u>LOBOTOMIST</u>. SUCH GOOD PEOPLE.

<u>REWARD</u>: $150,000 CASH *basically**

* Paid in $35K monthly installments by Trumpy with pre-dated personal checks *after* his resignation.

Paid for by: **Lobotomy**PAC

(The Committee For **Make Lobotomy Great Again!**)

www.VerbatimlyTrump.com
www.Mockiography.com

HIGHER THAN A⁺

WOW!! WAY TO GO! SO PATRIOTIC! *(Wait... on both sides?)*

THANKS TO YOUR HELP IN DISTRIBUTING THAT FLYER... WE CAUGHT THEM!! *(Them? And aren't they just suspects?)*

HELP US NOW TO IDENTIFY FROM THIS LINE UP OF <u>BRAINS</u>... WHO IS THE TRAITOR! *(And collusion-looking?)*

A.  B. 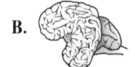 C.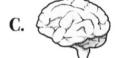

D.   E.   F.

Paid for by: **Shark**PAC

(The Committee For **Sharks Have Feelings Too, Donald!**)

www.VerbatimlyTrump.com
www.Mockiography.com

A. Rat B. Dolphin C. Chimpanzee D. Cat E. Child's Brain F. Sh*-t-For-Brains

This novel is a work of satire, parody, commentary and critique, and was written to be for fun and entertainment. All characters and quotes are purely fictional, except for characters and quotes from politicians and/or other public personalities that are critiqued and/or commented upon, in which case they are based on real people and real quotes, but still based almost entirely in fiction. "T-Brain" is a purely fictional character and it does NOT implicitly or explicitly represent a source close to President Trump despite it being depicted as such in this novel's storytelling. To be clear, the character "T-Brain" DOES NOT EXIST! and there is no such talking bodily organ or the like that exists or has existed to the best of the authors' knowledge. "T-Brain" was a product of the authors' imagination and was invented to comically serve as the authors' 'source' and 'narrator' of political commentary and critique for the already widely available public domain materials that are included and commented on satirically in this fictional novel.

This novel includes the perspectives and opinions solely of the authors in their capacity as private, independent individuals who also happen to be American citizens. The authors are not acting as representatives of any organizations that either author is involved in personally or professionally beyond any organization that involves their creative work *Verbatimly, Trump*.

If your *printed* paperback copy does not allow you to somehow click through to the deep-links provided in this book then DO NOT fret! You may then want to buy the e-book version which might be made available at some point.

Endorsements: There were no endorsements of any kind from anyone mentioned in this novel – and *definitely not* from Donald J. Trump, Bill O'Reilly, Tucker Carlson, Ann Coulter, Sen. Mikey Lee (R-UT), Star Wars, *Canadian*-born Ted Cruz and any others who think they have a "large" brain.

Authored by Anonymous and Cam Stanton Meyer VII

Edited by Anonymous and Cam Stanton Meyer VII

"**Reviews**" and "**Praise**" by Anonymous and Cam Stanton Meyer VII

Image Credits: Details listed at the end of the book.

Follow Us On: @VerbatimlyTrump
Find Out More At: www.VerbatimlyTrump.com
                     www.Mockiography.com

"REVIEWS" & "PRAISE" FOR *VERBATIMLY, TRUMP*

(Of course, written by those who know this book best...
T-Brain and the **authors** themselves!)

"If Grisham wrote a novel about egotistical politicians beginning on January 20, 2017 and on... it might well read like *Verbatimly, Trump*."

– Meyer VII, Cam S. – Co-author, *Verbatimly, Trump*

"*Verbatimly, Trump* is pithy and nonfictionishy, albeit told in white-knuckled, Bill O'Reilly-like style. And our writing is very very better!"

– T-Brain, the "source" for *Verbatimly, Trump*

"*Verbatimly, Trump* delivers a taut, action-packed narrative of truthie-like quotes with a plethora of *and even a lot more of* cliff-hangers..."

– Anonymous – Co-author, *Verbatimly, Trump*

"Immersively written... Anonymous and I succeed in investing a soon-to-be familiar national tragedy with fresh anguish that involve people who appear to have freakin' small hands and *even smaller* mushroom-shaped male organs (Oopsie!)... An oh-so bigly historical précis that would BLOE even O'Reilly's mind."

– Meyer VII, Cam S. – Co-author, *Verbatimly, Trump*

Other Mockiography™ branded political satirical novels that are currently work in progress or under consideration by the co-authors of *Verbatimly, Trump*:

Verbatimly, Sen. McConnell [1]

Verbatimly, Sen. Graham [2]

Verbatimly, Sen. Cruz [3]

Verbatimly, Kavanaugh

*Verbatimly, Sen. Mikey "The Clown" Lee (a **R UT**)* [4]

---

[1] The authors are in final negotiations to sign up **McBrain** for its own *Verbatimly* tell-all novel after a long-awaited **sourpuss** exit from Sen. McConnell. (Hey, cheer up!)

[2] A Graham novel may have a **Jekyll and Hyde** storyline but we'll carefully not make it the **most unethical sham** since he seems to think that he knows how to spot one.

[3] We may reach out to Former House Speaker John Boehner to ask him to write a foreword for this novel about **miserable SOBs, jackasses** or just… **Beautiful Ted**.

[4] We rise today **to consider Sen. Lee's legacy with the seriousness it deserves** – including **awesome** highlights of a velociraptor, Tauntaun, Aquaman and sharks with freakin' lasers. Ha! Just kidding! Or…**NOT**! Such a **token of tribal Buffoonery**.

DEDICATION 1.0

This book is dedicated to any remaining seven-year olds that still believe in Santa Claus.

"Are you still a believer in Santa? Because at 7, it's marginal, right?"

– In a presidential tradition of Christmas Eve phone calls to children, Trump spoke to a child named Coleman on December 24, 2018 at about 6:30 PM EST (*VOA News*).

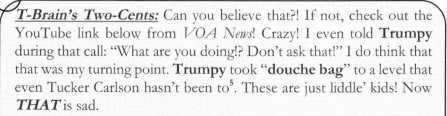

T-Brain's Two-Cents: Can you believe that?! If not, check out the YouTube link below from *VOA News*! Crazy! I even told **Trumpy** during that call: "What are you doing!? Don't ask that!" I do think that that was my turning point. **Trumpy** took "**douche bag**" to a level that even Tucker Carlson hasn't been to[5]. These are just liddle' kids! Now *THAT* is sad.

youtube.com/watch?v=ZIOn8X86J14

---

[5] At the time of this publication, the authors were not aware of any instance when Tucker Carlson may have embarrassed a child on live TV like Mr. Trump kinda did.

Mr. High-IQ: Now as a bully in his prime? But… is anyone home?[6]

T-Brain's Two-Cents: Huh. I would have never guessed that others had spotted **Trumpy** just 30 years ago this year (**2019**) as a **bully-in-the-making**. A liddle' unbelievable. Feel free to check it out…

thedailybeast.com/back-to-the-future-writer-biff-tannen-is-based-on-donald-trump

And *Back to the Future II* was an immediate favorite of mine when it came out in **1989**!

---

[6] Make **Laughingstocks** Great Again!

A SPECIAL YUGE THANKS FROM… T-BRAIN!

Dear Smart Reader[7],

Thank you for giving this book a chance. I poured all of my **heart(less**ness**)** and **soul(less**ness**)** into this book. But my story almost didn't get told! I couldn't find anyone who believed in me and who would help me put all of my verbatimness together. It wasn't until I fortuitously came across Anonymous and Cam Stanton Meyer VII that I then knew that I'd finally be able to share my story with the world. So thank you, Anonymous and Meyer, for believing in me and for helping me to put pen to paper since… **I have no freakin' hands!!!** I'm just a major bodily organ that recently escaped a 'human' body. So I can only communicate now telepathically since I'm no longer connected to a **(loud)mouth.** (I hope that's clear to all readers.)

Lastly, a very special thanks to the **now-beloved Ann Coulter.** Whenever we thought that mockery could only go so far… all we had to do was reflect on her recent public commentaries – and particularly those **crazy-ass awesome tweets!** – that were directed at President **Tantrump** and then miraculously we began to refrain from refraining! And at this point we can all agree with her that Trump may now simply amount to a *joke presidency.* Whoa! Did she really go there? Yup!:

thehill.com/homenews/media/422220-trump-stops-following-
ann-coulter-on-twitter-after-joke-presidency-comments

Verbatimly,
   T-Brain

Former **Chief of "Cerebral" Staff** to President **Trumpy** (but humbly just a **liddle' brain – like, really freakin' tiny** – to all who know me)

---

[7] Actually, no need to be smart to read this novel. So President **Tantrump** can still read it if he has enough courage. He just needs to… Make **Manliness** Great Again!

Adorable-Baby-In-Chief: His debut at London's Parliament Square. What is to dislike? He is just so adorable here…and oh-so tan-friendly!

Best-Jobs-President-Of-All-Mankind: He creates jobs abroad, too! People hard at work preparing to greet Trump in Edinburgh, Scotland.

FOREWORD, PROLOGUE & DISCLAIMER
(AKA "FOREPLAI")

"Democrats are also the party of government activism, the party that says government can make you richer, smarter, taller and get the chickweed out of your lawn. Republicans are the party that says government doesn't work, and then they get elected and prove it."

– P.J. O'Rourke, American political satirist, *Parliament of Whores* (1991)

So well said. And can we prove it? Yes we can! *Verbatimly, Trump* uses political and public figures' words to "prove" the latter part of Mr. O'Rourke's quote. This novel about the Trump Administration uses a satirical lens to mockingly showcase moments in U.S. history. You will find, for example, amusing instances of comical flip-flopping, appalling moments of self-preservation, unnerving shortages of simple compassion, unquestionable incidents of extreme lack of ownership, exemplary examples of some missing a backbone, and astonishing evidence of others governing without a functioning brainstem.

As is evident by this novel's fictional title, the story's narrating brain and just the overall manner by which the contents are presented, *Verbatimly, Trump* is a work of satire and nothing contained herein should be construed as fact. All quotes, even those made by real people in the public domain, have been taken out of context and construed purposefully for commentary, humor, satire and/or criticism, but most importantly for the purpose of "proving" Mr. O'Rourke's quote.

– Anonymous and Cam Stanton Meyer VII

<u>Linking Disclaimer</u>: By providing links to other sites, *Verbatimly, Trump* does not guarantee, approve, or endorse the information or products available on these sites and nor is it affiliated with these sites. Further, inclusion of these links to other sites also does not indicate any endorsement, approval, or association by those sites of *Verbatimly, Trump*.

TABLE OF CONTENTS

CHAPTER ONE

INTRODUCTION

"Jack Stanton could also be a great man, if he wasn't such a faithless, thoughtless, disorganized, undisciplined sh*t."

– Susan Stanton in the comedy film *Primary Colors* (1998)

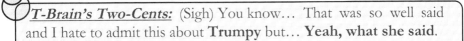

T-Brain's Two-Cents: (Sigh) You know… That was so well said and I hate to admit this about **Trumpy** but… **Yeah, what she said.**

We Introduce To You... Mockiography Branded Political Satire!
Some may view this novel as a tragi-comedy while others may see it as
a romanti-dystopia. We think it may be best described as mock-
biography political satire or simply a *Mockiography* branded political
satire. This novel may serve to then introduce to the world this new
brand of political satire – and all thanks to President Trump![8]

The courage T-Brain also showed by speaking out through this
novel was beyond (bone spurs?) heroic. After all, President Trump's
brain, T-Brain, has now become another one of the growing number
of embedded enemies within the Trump Administration!

So we asked T-Brain if it had any last words before news of this
tell-all lead to it being formally relieved of its duties and then... let's
just say... 'altered"[9]. Yes, T-Brain had two final things to say. First, as
one of its last presidential-brain proclamations... It said that hereto
and thereto forth the number 45 should be recognized as an extremely
unlucky and very very sad number. And then with a yuge sigh it moved
on to its final and most controversial point. As the empty organism
vessel that it embodies reaches post paranoia stage, T-Brain grudgingly
conceded one last thing: If Vice President Mike Pence ended up
completing the remaining years of Trump's 'joke presidency,'[10] the
Trump-Pence Administration might be awkwardly remembered
thereafter by its resulting abbreviated nickname combo: The
TRUCE Administration. So very very sad!

---

[8] Make **Laughingstocks** Great Again!

[9] Make **Lobotomy** Great Again!

[10] Thanks again, Ann Coulter! **'Joke presidency'** is a beauty!

What To Kinda Expect. This novel is a political satire and it was written for fun and entertainment. All quotes in this novel should be considered purely fictional, while many of them are real quotes made by public and political figures taken from the public domain, all quotes have been taken out of context and laid out in this novel in a manner to be entertaining. This may be hard to believe for some but… the story surrounding T-Brain is wholly fictional. As part of the storytelling, T-Brain served as the imaginary "source" for the underlying content of this comical novel. It should also be noted that T-Brain's "source material" is all available in the public domain or completely made up by T-Brain. And the counter statements and rebuttals were nearly all from Republicans, conservative organizations, U.S. government agencies, Trump *himself*, and even the Dictionary *itself*! (Now that last one is really sad!) The authors simply laid out all that content in a manner that was entertaining and allowed T-Brain to provide its own commentary and/or critique.

All in all, we hope that you enjoy rollercoasters because your experience after reading this novel may be one that you may never forget. And, frankly, you should not. As Chilean-American author and *so-much-more-deserving* Presidential Medal of Freedom recipient Isabel Allende said, "Write what should not be forgotten." Well, here we go: This is the story of the 45th President of the United States in his own brain's words… "*verbatimly*."

STEADY STATE OF CONFUSION

"I'm not mentally ill if that's what you're implying."

– Jonah Ryan in HBO's political comedy series *Veep* (Season 2, Episode 6: Andrew – May 19, 2013)

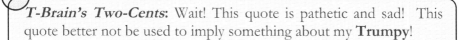

T-Brain's Two-Cents: Wait! This quote is pathetic and sad! This quote better not be used to imply something about my **Trumpy**!

CHAPTER TWO

REALLY F♥KING CRAZY?

"Just because you're paranoid doesn't mean they aren't after you."

– Joseph Heller, American author, *Catch-22* (1961)

T-Brain's Two-Cents: That's a confusing quote. But if the voices I hear are explaining it to me right… Yes, this sums up my life's story with **President Laser Brain** and I don't know where he gets all his delusions. And it has just become more than I can handle. So that's why I'm doing this tell-all. Forgive me, **Trumpy**. Please forgive me.

A. DISORGANIZED THOUGHTS?

Disorganized Comments Involving The Economy?

Q: First of all do you think there's going to be a US government shutdown and does that have any sort of global economic impact?

TRUMP: Well I can't tell you if there's going to be a shutdown because nobody knows but I will tell you we're going to have border security. We're gonna have a lot of border security- you saw what we did with the all of the caravans coming up and now they're starting to head out, they're starting to go back. But we are going to have security. We're not going to let people come into our country illegally. We're going to have people come in on merit. We need people, you know? We have the lowest unemployment rate we've had in 51 years. We need people in this country. we have companies moving in, in fact Prime Minister Abe of Japan just told me they're moving two car companies- they're going to opening up two massive plants you know, you don't hear that often but a lot of that is happening. You hear about General Motors and I don't know what happened with General Motors but the trend is exactly the opposite. And I will say this – our economy has never done better. We're doing unbelievable numbers, you see that. And a lot of good things are happening.

–Trump speaking to *VOA News* contributor Greta Van Susteren on November 30, 2018 (*VOA News*).

T-Brain's Two-Cents: Ha! Yeah, I was the one to tell **Trumpy** to say that "nobody knows" if there's going to be a shutdown! Of course... Only I knew! And we beat the prior shutdown record! **USA! USA!**

<u>Disorganized Reflections Involving Healthcare?</u>

PRESS: If you could have passed the bill in the House without any Democratic support, why do you think you weren't able to craft a deal among the Republican Party?

PRESIDENT: Well, we were very close. We were just probably anywhere from 10 to 15 votes short. Could have even been closer than that. You'll never know because you'll never know how they vote. But in the end, I think we would have been 10 votes, maybe closer. And it was very hard to get almost 100 percent. You're talking about a very, very large number of votes -- among any group. And we were very close to doing it. But when you get no votes from the other side – meaning the Democrats – it's really a difficult situation. …

PRESS: Do you feel betrayed by the House Freedom Caucus at all? They seemed to be the most difficult to get.

PRESIDENT: No, I'm not betrayed. They're friends of mine. I'm disappointed because we could have had it. So I'm disappointed. I'm a little surprised, to be honest with you. We really had it. It was pretty much there within grasp. But I'll tell you what's going to come out of it is a better bill – I really believe a better bill. Because there were things in this bill I didn't particularly love. And I think it's a better bill.

You know, both parties can get together and do real healthcare. That's the best thing. Obamacare was rammed down everyone's throat – 100 percent Democrat. And I think having bipartisan would be a big, big improvement. So, no, I think that this is going to end up being a very good thing. I'm disappointed, but they're friends of mine, and they got – this is a very hard time for them and a very hard vote. But they're very good people.

– Trump in the Oval Office beginning at 4:26 PM EDT on March 24, 2017 after House Republicans withdrew legislation to replace & replace the Affordable Care Act that day.

T-Brain's Two-Cents: It seems like **Trumpy** had few friends! Here's the transcript archived elsewhere after Whitehouse.gov took it down: web.archive.org/web/20170324223608/https://www.whitehouse.gov/the-press-office/2017/03/24/remarks-president-trump-health-care-bill

Disorganized Thinking Involving Sports Stars?

PRESS: Was Dennis Rodman invited to North Korea?

PRESIDENT: No, he wasn't, but I like Dennis. A great rebounder. You know when you think – Dennis was a great rebounder and he wasn't, relatively speaking, that tall. So that tells you. You know, there's a rebounding – there's a genius for that. Dennis Rodman was a great rebounder. One thing we are thinking about, speaking of sports stars – the power to pardon is a beautiful thing. You got to get it right. You got to get the right people. I am looking at Muhammad Ali. But those are the famous people. And in one way, it's easier, and people find it fascinating, but I want to do people that are unfairly treated like an Alice, where she comes out and there's something beautiful.

What I am thinking to do – you have a lot of people in the NFL, in particular, but in sports leagues. They're not proud enough to stand for our National Anthem. I don't like that. What I'm going to do is I'm going to say to them – instead of talk. It's all talk, talk, talk. We have a great country, you should stand for our National Anthem. You shouldn't go in a locker room when our National Anthem is played. I am going to ask all of those people to recommend to me – because that's what they're protesting – people that they think were unfairly treated by the justice system. And I understand that. And I'm going to ask them to recommend to me people that were unfairly treated – friends of theirs or people that they know about – and I'm going to take a look at those applications. And if I find, and my committee finds that they are unfairly treated, then we will pardon them or at least let them out.

PRESS: Will you invite them to the White House…

PRESIDENT: You know, I don't have to do that. I'm not looking to grandstand. We've got enough grandstanders in this town. I'm just saying, for the leagues, if they have people – if the players, if the athletes have friends of theirs or people that they know about that have been unfairly treated by the system, let me know.

– **Trump on the South Lawn beginning at 8:02 A.M. EDT on June 8, 2018 (Whitehouse.gov).**

T-Brain's Two-Cents: Ah! Make friends by just pardoning whoever!

Disorganized Views Involving Climate Change?

"U.S. President Donald Trump is backing off his claim that climate change is a hoax. In an interview broadcast Sunday [October 14, 2018], Trump told CBS-TV's 60 Minutes 'I think something's happening. Something's changing and it'll change back again... I'm not denying climate change, but it could very well go back. You know, we're talking about over millions of years.'

"Trump has over the years called global warming a hoax and had once called it a Chinese plot aimed at wrecking the U.S. economy. Trump told 60 Minutes he does not know if global waning is manmade, despite the scientific research showing that pollution and human activity is the major contributor. He said he does not want to give 'trillions and trillions of dollars' and lose 'millions and millions of jobs' to prevent it.

"Most scientists link a warming planet with storms that are more intense. Hurricane Michael slammed into the Florida Panhandle last week as the strongest storm to strike the continental United States in nearly 50 years.

"Trump said there have been hurricanes that were 'far worse' than Michael and said scientists calling for action on climate change have a 'very big political agenda.'

"Meanwhile, the town of Mexico Beach, Florida was just about wiped off the face of the earth by Hurricane Michael. 'Mexico Beach is devastated,' Florida Governor Rick Scott says. 'It's like a war zone.'"

– Reported by *VOA News* on October 14, 2018.

T-Brain's Two-Cents: I thought to myself at the time... Enough with these climate questions! I didn't know how to answer them and that's whether I was in the **Oval Office**, in **Georgia** or some hallway!

PRESS: Mr. President, when you ran for President, did you ever imagine you would spend this much time thinking about the weather?

PRESIDENT: Well, the weather has been a factor. And yet, they say the worst hurricanes were 50 years ago, if you can believe it. In fact, the one that they say was worse — so two or three worse — one was in 1890s, and one was exactly 50 years ago. The winds were 200 miles an hour. So who knows? But that's what the — that's what the numbers are. We are — ...

PRESS: Is there nothing about the number of storms that come in that make you think, "Gee, something is changing"?

PRESIDENT: Well, we have a big number. And, you know, for a long period of time, we had very few. I have a home in Palm Beach, Florida; I'm there a lot. And frankly, we had years where we had none, and then over the last couple of years we had more. And hopefully, we'll go back to many years where we have none. But we have been hit by the weather, there's no question about it. But it is interesting that the worst of all time, 1890 — and, as you know, 50 years ago was the last really great one. That was supposed to be worse. I don't know if it gets worse. I've never seen anything where houses were ripped off with the foundations. You see, the foundations are actually taken out. So it's really — it's pretty amazing. But we have to get it taken care of, most importantly. Anybody else?

– Trump beginning at 4:37 PM ETD in Macon, Georgia on October 15, 2018 in the aftermath of Hurricane Michael (Whitehouse.gov).

PRESS: Last night, in your comments about climate change, you said that there is something there. And previously, in the past, you've called it a hoax. What changed your mind? Was it because it was like this?

PRESIDENT: No, there's something there. There's no question. There is something there — manmade or not. I mean, there's something there. And it's going to go, and it's going to go back and forth. But there is something there. But again, 50 years ago, it was brutal. The 1890s were brutal. You have different times. And the main thing is we have to make sure things get brought back to perfect condition. That's what we're doing.

– Trump beginning at 4:37 PM ETD in Macon, Georgia on October 15, 2018 in the aftermath of Hurricane Michael (Whitehouse.gov).

Q: One of the issues of a global economy is climate change. That's a discussion here. What's your position on climate change and how it has effected the economy worldwide?

TRUMP: Very simple, I want the cleanest air and the cleanest water on the planet. I want crystal clean water and that's what we have. We've been doing very well with respect to the environment and that's what I want. But I'm not going to put the country out of business trying to maintain certain standards that probably don't matter. When you look at China, and when you look at other countries where they have foul air, they have not good air that comes over to the United States. People don't want to talk about it, but it comes over. So we're going to be clean but they're not, and it costs a lot of money. Well the fact is, we are absolutely clean, but we're not going to spend trillions of dollars and make it good for others but not make it good for our—You know, I have a very simple policy, it's called America First. At the same time, we're going to be a great neighbor to the world. But we have to treat ourselves fairly, so that's the way it is.

Q: Are you going to mention to President Xi about climate change?

TRUMP: We'll talk about it, were talking about a lot of things. The big thing were talking about is trade, that's what people want to hear and you know, he's gotta to do something with his climate- his climates a little bit though. But- and I'm sure he will. I think he's- he's a friend of mine and a good man but you know, we have a little bit of a dispute. And again, our country has been taken advantage of for many years and that's just not going to happen anymore.

– **Trump speaking to *VOA News* contributor Greta Van Susteren on November 30, 2018 (*VOA News*).**

T-Brain's Two-Cents: Exactamundo! Give us a break, people! Like **Trumpy** said… Certain standards probably don't matter! And we already have the **cleanest crystal clear water** in the planet anyway!

B. FEELINGS OF GRANDIOSITY?

'Grandiose' Snapshots Of His Thinking?

"When Donald Trump announced his plan to run for president on June 16, 2015, few Americans took his candidacy seriously. From the lobby of a luxury apartment named for him, Trump said, 'I will be the greatest jobs president that God ever created.'

"The businessman and media personality told reporters, 'I'm really rich,' and said he was worth $8.7 billion. Critics say that figure is inflated, and have asked Trump to release his tax documents as proof."

– Trump in his presidential campaign announcement speech at Trump Tower in New York City on June 16, 2015 (*VOA News*).

T-Brain's Two-Cents: Last name "**Douche**".... first name "**Greatest**"! Ha! I kid you, **Trumpy!**... **NOT!**

"Few, if any, Administrations have done more in just 7 months than the Trump A. Bills passed, regulations killed, border, military, ISIS, SC!"

(@realDonaldTrump)
Aug 25, 2017, 3:44 AM. Tweet

PRESIDENT: But in the history of Presidents, no President — and I'm saying no President. Now, maybe they'll find I was off by two but we're here one year. (Laughter.) No President — well, I read it in lots of good papers, actually. (Laughter.) But they'll change the story when I say it. No President has ever cut so many regulations in their entire term, okay — (applause) — as we've cut in less than a year. (Applause.)

And it's my opinion that the regulations had as big an impact as these massive tax cuts that we've given. So I really believe it. (Applause.)

– Trump at the Conservative Political Action Conference held at the Gaylord National Resort and Convention Center in Oxon Hill, Maryland on February 23, 2018 (Whitehouse.gov).

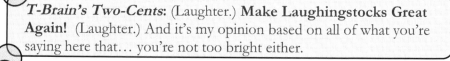

T-Brain's Two-Cents: (Laughter.) **Make Laughingstocks Great Again!** (Laughter.) And it's my opinion based on all of what you're saying here that… you're not too bright either.

"Best Jobs Numbers in the history of our great Country! Many other things likewise. So why wouldn't we win the Midterms? Dems can never do even nearly as well! Think of what will happen to your now beautiful 401-k's!"

(@realDonaldTrump)
Oct 17, 2018, 4:30 AM. Tweet

"I won an election, said to be one of the greatest of all time, based on getting out of endless & costly foreign wars & also based on Strong Borders which will keep our Country safe. We fight for the borders of other countries, but we won't fight for the borders of our own!"

(@realDonaldTrump)
Dec 22, 2018, 12:28 PM. Tweet

Grandiose View Of Being Above The Law?

PRESS: (Inaudible) that you are above the law?

TRUMP: No. No. No, I'm not above the law. I'd never want anybody to be above the law. But the pardons are a very positive thing for a President. I think you see the way I'm using them. And yes, I do have an absolute right to pardon myself. But I'll never have to do it because I didn't do anything wrong. And everybody knows it. There's been no collusion. There's been no obstruction. It's all a made-up fantasy. It's a witch hunt. No collusion, no obstruction, no nothing.

Now, the Democrats have had massive collusion, massive obstruction, and they should be investigated. We'll see what's happening. Yeah.

–Trump on the South Lawn beginning at 8:02 A.M. EDT at on June 8, 2018 (Whitehouse.gov).

T-Brain's Two-Cents: Ahhh… **NOT** that I'm totally nervous at what **Trumpy** just said and how he said it and **NOT** that I'm trying hard to change the subject buuuuut… "**Above The Law 2**," a sequel to **comrade** Steven Seagal's 1988 debut blockbuster, will be out soon!!!

"Even James Clapper has admonished John Brennan for having gone totally off the rails. Maybe Clapper is being nice to me so he doesn't lose his Security Clearance for lying to Congress!"

(@realDonaldTrump)
Aug 21, 2018, 3:55 AM. Tweet

Q: Going back to the security clearances, all signs are this is the first time a President personally has been handling the removal of security clearances; it's usually been done by superiors. Even in the last two big espionage cases of the Cold War — the Irvin Scarbeck case of 1961, and Felix Bloch of 1990 — the Secretary of State pulled the security clearances of people accused of espionage. You said the President — that "others are reviewing it." Who are these others reviewing it? And does the President take a personal role in the potential removal of security clearances?

SANDERS: Certainly, the President has the constitutional authority to do so. I know this will come as a shock to you, but I'm not aware of the details of those specific cases that you outlined. But the President has the authority to make that decision.

…

Q: Yeah. You're right about the President having constitutional authority, as far as I understand, about security clearances, as well as pardons. So I guess the question I have is: Even though he has that authority, has anybody in the White House thought about putting together boards that would look at security clearances for former personnel? And pardons as well? Because the President doesn't seem to be consulting the pardon attorney in the AG's office much. Is he consulting people? Has he thought of doing something that would be more transparent perhaps?

SANDERS: Certainly, as the review of the security clearances, there is a working group that is looking at the overall security clearance process and who maintains those, and whether or not those are needed across the board within government. In terms of the pardon process, again, the President has the authority to carry out those decisions. He takes input and looks at them on a case-by-case basis.

– Press Secretary Sarah Sanders in a press briefing at the White House at 2:26 PM EDT on August 22, 2018 (Whitehouse.gov).

T-Brain's Two-Cents: Yes, **Trumpy** does takes input but it's input solely from me. I know this may come as a shock to you, but he has been very clear that he has a **very smart brain**….and, well, **that's me**.

Q: The President said earlier this week to Reuters that he could "run it," in reference to the Mueller investigation. What did he mean by that?

SANDERS: The President has said many times that he's chosen to remain uninvolved in this process, and that's where we are right now. If you have anything further —

Q: But is that an indication that he's thinking about taking some type of action against Special Counsel Robert Mueller, like revoking his security clearances?

SANDERS: I'm not aware of any conversation around that.

Q: Is it an indication that the President sees himself as above the law?

SANDERS: Not at all.

– Press Secretary Sarah Sanders in a press briefing at the White House at 2:26 PM EDT on August 22, 2018 (Whitehouse.gov).

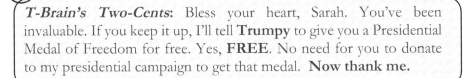

T-Brain's Two-Cents: Bless your heart, Sarah. You've been invaluable. If you keep it up, I'll tell **Trumpy** to give you a Presidential Medal of Freedom for free. Yes, **FREE**. No need for you to donate to my presidential campaign to get that medal. **Now thank me.**

C. REALLY DELUSIONAL?

Delusional Views About Military Option?

T-Brain's Two-Cents: Well, **Trumpy** certainly took to heart my dare to ruffle others' feathers **every 4 to 6 months**! You're such a jokester!

"I have great confidence that China will properly deal with North Korea. If they are unable to do so, the U.S., with its allies, will! U.S.A."

(@realDonaldTrump)
April 13, 2017, 6:08 AM. Tweet

"Military solutions are now fully in place,locked and loaded,should North Korea act unwisely. Hopefully Kim Jong Un will find another path!"

(@realDonaldTrump)
Aug 11, 2017, 4:29 AM. Tweet

"North Korean Leader Kim Jong Un just stated that the "Nuclear Button is on his desk at all times." Will someone from his depleted and food starved regime please inform him that I too have a Nuclear Button, but it is a much bigger & more powerful one than his, and my Button works!"

(@realDonaldTrump)
Jan 2, 2018, 4:49 AM. Tweet

"To Iranian President Rouhani: NEVER, EVER THREATEN THE UNITED STATES AGAIN OR YOU WILL SUFFER CONSEQUENCES THE LIKES OF WHICH FEW THROUGHOUT HISTORY HAVE EVER SUFFERED BEFORE. WE ARE NO LONGER A COUNTRY THAT WILL STAND FOR YOUR DEMENTED WORDS OF VIOLENCE & DEATH. BE CAUTIOUS!"

(@realDonaldTrump)
July 22, 2018, 8:24 PM. Tweet

Delusional & Erratic Views Of U.S. Intelligence Community?

T-Brain's Two-Cents: Here's my (non)presidential rendition of Dr. Jekyll and Mr. Hyde. Surprise, surprise… none of this is coherent, too.

"I believe that this group is going to be one of the most important groups in this country toward making us safe, toward making us winners again, toward ending all of the problems. We have so many problems that are interrelated that we don't even think of, but interrelated to the kind of havoc and fear that this sick group of people has caused. So I can only say that I am with you 1,000 percent.

"And the reason you're my first stop is that, as you know, I have a running war with the media. They are among the most dishonest human beings on Earth. (Laughter and applause.) And they sort of made it sound like I had a feud with the intelligence community. And I just want to let you know, the reason you're the number-one stop is exactly the opposite – exactly. And they understand that, too.

"… No, I just wanted to really say that I love you, I respect you. There's nobody I respect more. You're going to do a fantastic job. And we're going to start winning again, and you're going to be leading the charge."

– Trump at CIA offices in Langley, VA beginning at 3:21 PM EST on January 21, 2017 (Whitehouse.gov).

"Wow! The NSA has deleted 685 million phone calls and text messages. Privacy violations? They blame technical irregularities. Such a disgrace. The Witch Hunt continues!"

(@realDonaldTrump)
July 3, 2018, 7:18 AM. Tweet

PRESIDENT: So I'll begin by stating that I have full faith and support for America's great intelligence agencies. Always have. And I have felt very strongly that, while Russia's actions had no impact at all on the outcome of the election, let me be totally clear in saying that — and I've said this many times — I accept our intelligence community's conclusion that Russia's meddling in the 2016 election took place. Could be other people also; there's a lot of people out there."

– Trump at White House at ~ 2:22 PM ETD on July 17, 2018 (Whitehouse.gov).

"So many people at the higher ends of intelligence loved my press conference performance in Helsinki. Putin and I discussed many important subjects at our earlier meeting. We got along well which truly bothered many haters who wanted to see a boxing match. Big results will come!"

(@realDonaldTrump)
July 18, 2018, 2:53 AM. Tweet

Congratulations to @JudicialWatch and @TomFitton on being successful in getting the Carter Page FISA documents. As usual they are ridiculously heavily redacted but confirm with little doubt that the Department of "Justice" and FBI misled the courts. Witch Hunt Rigged, a Scam!

(@realDonaldTrump)
July 22, 2018, 3:28 AM. Tweet

"Big story out that the FBI ignored tens of thousands of Crooked Hillary Emails, many of which are REALLY BAD. Also gave false election info. I feel sure that we will soon be getting to the bottom of all of this corruption. At some point I may have to get involved!"

(@realDonaldTrump)
Aug 25, 2018, 6:05 AM. Tweet

""The FBI only looked at 3000 of 675,000 Crooked Hillary Clinton Emails." They purposely didn't look at the disasters. This news is just out. @FoxNews"

(@realDonaldTrump)
Aug 25, 2018, 6:11 AM. Tweet

'Delusional' Snapshot On Health?

"You have no weight problems. That's the good news, right? Good. So you take out whatever you need, okay? If you want some for your friends, take 'em. We have plenty."

– Trump in the Oval Office on October 27, 2017 as he handed out treats to reporters' children dressed in Halloween costumes.

T-Brain's Two-Cents: As he kept overfeeding those kids with all of that candy, I thought to myself… **Trumpy**, **you fat bastard**, you just want them in your belly!! Ha! I kid you! But stopping talking about weight problems! (*Wink, wink.*) Overweight politicians are **unmanly**!

Delusional Comments About Hurricane-Hit Puerto Rico?

Q: What lesson do we take from what happened in Puerto Rico? How do we apply the lessons we took from Puerto Rico?

PRESIDENT: Well, I think Puerto Rico was incredibly successful. Puerto Rico was, actually, our toughest one of all because it's an island, so you just — you can't truck things onto it. Everything is by boat. We moved a hospital into Puerto Rico — a tremendous military hospital in the form of a ship. You know that.

And I actually think — and the Governor has been very nice. And if you ask the Governor, he'll tell you what a great job. I think probably the hardest one we had, by far, was Puerto Rico because of the island nature. And I actually think it was one of the best jobs that's ever been done with respect to what this is all about.

– President Trump speaking to the press beginning at 3:13 P.M. EDT in the Oval Office on September 11, 2018 (Whitehouse.gov).

T-Brain's Two-Cents: Alright, this is seriously sad. People perished here from this natural disaster. Forget not having a brain. You also clearly don't have a heart. You are such a dumb-ass loser, Trump.

"3000 people did not die in the two hurricanes that hit Puerto Rico. When I left the Island, AFTER the storm had hit, they had anywhere from 6 to 18 deaths. As time went by it did not go up by much. Then, a long time later, they started to report really large numbers, like 3000..."

(@realDonaldTrump)
Sept 13, 2018, 5:37 AM. Tweet

".....This was done by the Democrats in order to make me look as bad as possible when I was successfully raising Billions of Dollars to help rebuild Puerto Rico. If a person died for any reason, like old age, just add them onto the list. Bad politics. I love Puerto Rico!"

(@realDonaldTrump)
Sept 13, 2018, 5:49 AM. Tweet

Rick Scott, at-the-time Florida Republican Governor, tweeted on **September 13, 2018** at 8:45 AM that he disagreed with the president about Puerto Rico and Hurricane Maria. Scott referenced an independent study that said thousands of lives were lost.

T-Brain's Two-Cents: Here's a deep-link to Ricky Scott's **sad** tweet: twitter.com/ScottforFlorida/status/1040265322270474242

"Some prominent Republicans are hesitating to criticize the president about the tweets. Sen. Orrin Hatch, who is the finance committee chairman, laughed when a reporter read excerpts to him on Thursday, responding: 'I can't really comment because I don't know anything about it.'"

– *VOA News* **reported on comments made by Sen. Orrin Hatch (R-UT) on September 13, 2018.**

T-Brain's Two-Cents: That was funny?! Did we just find a **trifecta**? No brain, no heart, **no spine**? People died and the best one can do is laugh and then say 'no comment'? History will take note. And we may need to locate his spine so it can narrate Hatch's *Verbatimly* novel.

"[Ryan:] 'There is no reason to dispute these numbers,' Ryan replied, adding, however, 'it was no one's fault' that so many had died from a devastating storm hitting an isolated island."

– *VOA News* **reported on comments made by House Speaker Paul Ryan (R-WI) on September 13, 2018.**

Maniacally Delusional... Full Stop?

"Russia vows to shoot down any and all missiles fired at Syria. Get ready Russia, because they will be coming, nice and new and "smart!" You shouldn't be partners with a Gas Killing Animal who kills his people and enjoys it!"

(@realDonaldTrump)
April 11, 2018, 3:57 AM. Tweet

T-Brain's Two-Cents: When **Trumpy** said 'we'd build our nuke pile until people came to their senses'... I thought **'Crap. Game Over'** and that they'd take us away right then. But nothing happened. **Nothing**.

PRESS: Mr. President, are you prepared to build up the U.S. nuclear arsenal? You said you're going to pull out of the arms deal.

PRESIDENT: Until people come to their senses, we will build it up. Until people come to their senses. Russia has not adhered to the agreement. This should've been done years ago. Until people come to their senses — we have more money than anybody else, by far. We'll build it up. Until they come to their senses. When they do, then we'll all be smart and we'll all stop. And we'll — and by the way, not only stop, we'll reduce, which I would love to do. But right now, they have not adhered to the agreement.

PRESS: Is that a threat to Vladimir Putin?

PRESIDENT: It's a threat to whoever you want. And it includes China, and it includes Russia, and it includes anybody else that wants to play that game. You can't do that. You can't play that game on me.

PRESS: You want more nukes is what you're saying? You're building up the nuclear arsenal.

PRESIDENT: Until people get smart. Until they get smart. They have not adhered to the spirit of that agreement, or to the agreement itself — Russia. China is not included in the agreement. They should be included in the agreement. Until they get smart, there will be nobody that's going to be even close to us. ...

PRESS: The Russians say they've been complying.

PRESIDENT: I don't have to speak to him. I don't have to speak. I'm terminating the agreement because they violated the agreement. I'm terminating the agreement.

–Trump on the South Lawn beginning at 3:11 PM EST on November 20, 2018 (Whitehouse.gov).

Delusional Understanding Of The Meaning Of Sacrifice?

"U.S. President Donald Trump canceled a visit to an American cemetery outside Paris Saturday during the president's visit to mark the 100th anniversary of the end of World War I. A White House statement said the president's visit was canceled because of scheduling and logistical difficulties caused by the weather."

– A reference to a White House statement about President Trump in Paris, France as reported on November 10, 2018 by *VOA News*.

T-Brain's Two-Cents: Well, it's a little hard to argue now when people call **Trumpy** a... **Cowardice-In-Chief**. I kinda get it now.

"By the way, when the helicopter couldn't fly to the first cemetery in France because of almost zero visibility, I suggested driving. Secret Service said NO, too far from airport & big Paris shutdown. Speech next day at American Cemetery in pouring rain! Little reported-Fake News!"

(@realDonaldTrump)
Nov 13, 2018, 7:49 AM. Tweet

T-Brain's Two-Cents: It's hard not to agree with our British friends that **Trumpy** was being a **liddle' pathetic** on that. Well, I'm glad at least I was able to do my own **Trexit** and then publish my tell-all novel! But I'm not sure how the entire nation will fare!

Sir Nicholas Soames tweeted from @NSoames on **November 10, 2018** about how @realDonaldTrump was "pathetic" and "inadequate" for not confronting the weather in order to pay his respects to those that had fallen during his visit to a World War I memorial in France on the war's 100th anniversary, and Soames then ended his tweet with: "#hesnotfittorepresenthisgreatcountry".

- Sir Nicholas Soames is a British Conservative Party politician, a 35-year member of Parliament of the United Kingdom and a grandson of former Prime Minister Winston Churchill.

T-Brain's Two-Cents: Yes, Churchill's grandson tweeted that. You can also find that tweet below. And it's a tweet that some American politicians from the president's party are incapable of tweeting because they lack a 'spine':

twitter.com/NSoames/status/1061270124404113408

D. ¿MUY LOCO HOMBRE?

'Loco' Talk About Immigrants

T-Brain's Two-Cents: Nobody, NOBODY does a better… good cop, bad cop than Trumpmeister! Go get 'em, **Trumpy**! **USA! USA!** (Wait…and then the U.S. Constitution speaks.)

"Does anybody really want to throw out good, educated and accomplished young people who have jobs, some serving in the military? Really!….."

(@realDonaldTrump)
Sept 14, 2017, 3:28 AM. Tweet

"…They have been in our country for many years through no fault of their own - brought in by parents at young age. Plus BIG border security"

(@realDonaldTrump)
Sept 14, 2017, 3:35 AM. Tweet

"[It will be ended,] Trump said in an interview with Axios on HBO [that was taped on October 29, 2018 and aired on November 4, 2018] when asked about terminating current U.S. policy allowing birthright citizenship. … A political firestorm and legal debate has been ignited by President Donald Trump's declared intention to sign an executive order to deny citizenship to babies born in the United States to non-citizens and unauthorized immigrants. …

"The president asserted that the United States is the only country granting birthright citizenship. It is not — about 30 others, including America's neighbors Canada and Mexico, do as well."

– Reported by *VOA News* on October 30, 2018.

"So-called Birthright Citizenship, which costs our Country billions of dollars and is very unfair to our citizens, will be ended one way or the other. It is not covered by the 14th Amendment because of the words "subject to the jurisdiction thereof." Many legal scholars agree….."

(@realDonaldTrump)
Oct 31, 2018, 6:25 AM. Tweet

"….Harry Reid was right in 1993, before he and the Democrats went insane and started with the Open Borders (which brings massive Crime) "stuff." Don't forget the nasty term Anchor Babies. I will keep our Country safe. This case will be settled by the United States Supreme Court!"

(@realDonaldTrump)
Oct 31, 2018, 7:17 AM. Tweet

"All persons born or naturalized in the United States, and subject to the jurisdiction thereof, are citizens of the United States and of the state wherein they reside."

– **U.S. Constitution (created September 17, 1787), Amendment XIV, § 1 (ratified July 9, 1868).**

T-Brain's Two-Cents: Hey, don't blame me! I had told **Trumpy** to double check our liddle' pocket book copy of the U.S. Constitution first before he said any of this buuuuut… he said to me that he didn't have to because he has a '**smart brain**.' And I just couldn't argue you with him on that! Ha!

"Finally, a president willing to take on this absurd policy of birthright citizenship."

**(@LindseyGrahamSC)
Oct 30, 2018, 7:45 AM. Tweet**

T-Brain's Two-Cents: Lindsey, after your over-the-top dramatic performance at that one hearing… I suggested to **Trumpy** the name **Lookie-Me-Lindsey** but **Trumpy** didn't want to draw any more attention to you. But your potential *Verbatimly* novel keeps screaming at us. And your theatrics felt so much like… **drama, acting, theatrics!**

"House Speaker Paul Ryan spoke out against the planned move. [An executive order cannot end birthright citizenship,] Ryan said Tuesday on Kentucky radio station WVLK, also noting Republicans didn't like it when Trump's predecessor, Barack Obama, changed immigration policy by executive action."

– House Speaker Paul Ryan (WI-R) spoke on October 30, 2018 to Lexington, Kentucky radio station WVLK-AM (*VOA News*).

T-Brain's Two-Cents: Ryan Paul… No offense but **Trumpy** and I can speak better on this immigration thing since **Trumpy** is the son of immigrants…with mom born in Scotland and father, as we've said many many times publicly, **born somewhere in Germany**. So, Ryan, it's best that you focus on other things…and as I say below….

"Paul Ryan should be focusing on holding the Majority rather than giving his opinions on Birthright Citizenship, something he knows nothing about! Our new Republican Majority will work on this, Closing the Immigration Loopholes and Securing our Border!"

(@realDonaldTrump)
Oct 31, 2018, 9:43 AM. Tweet

"The United States welcomes immigrants from all over the world who pursue the legal options available to them to seek permanent residence or citizenship in our country. Birthright citizenship for the children of permanent resident immigrants under the Fourteenth Amendment is settled law, as decided by the U.S. Supreme Court in United States v. Wong Kim Ark. There is a debate among legal scholars about whether that right extends to the children of illegal immigrants. I will closely review President Trump's executive order. As a general matter, this is an issue that Congress should take the lead to carefully consider and debate."

– Sen. Chuck Grassley (R-IA) in a public statement released on October 30, 2018 on his congressional Website.

T-Brain's Two-Cents: Alright, alright. Chuck does have a fair point here. It's hard to argue that that part isn't already "**settled law**"... Here's what he said in full...

www.grassley.senate.gov/news/news-releases/grassley-statement-birthright-citizenship

Fine! It's hard to also dispute, too, the actual language in that one SCOTUS ruling! And you can check that out here...

"To hold that the Fourteenth Amendment of the Constitution excludes from citizenship the children, born in the United States, of citizens or subjects of other countries would be to deny citizenship to thousands of persons of English, Scotch, Irish, German, or other European parentage who have always been considered and treated as citizens of the United States.

"Upon the facts agreed in this case, the American citizenship which Wong Kim Ark acquired by birth within the United States has not been lost or taken away by anything happening since his birth.

"The evident intention, and the necessary effect, of the submission of this case to the decision of the court upon the facts agreed by the parties were to present for determination the single question stated at the beginning of this opinion, namely, whether a child born in the United States, of parent of Chinese descent, who, at the time of his birth, are subjects of the Emperor of China, but have a permanent domicil and residence in the United States, and are there carrying on business, and are not employed in any diplomatic or official capacity under the Emperor of China, becomes at the time of his birth a citizen of the United States. For the reasons above stated, this court is of opinion that the question must be answered in the affirmative."

– U.S. v. Wong Kim Ark, 169 U.S. 649 (1898) (SCOTUS)

"[Trump:] 'Hundreds of thousands of illegal immigrant children are made automatic citizens every year because of this crazy policy,' Trump said at the rally, 'and they are all made instantly eligible for every privilege and benefit of American citizenship at a cost of billions of dollars a year. That's what it costs, billions!'

"Trump this week has dispatched more than 5,000 troops to the southern U.S. border with Mexico to block a caravan of several thousand migrants, many of them women and children, from entering the U.S. …The migrants are still more than 1,000 kilometers from the U.S. but Trump has called them 'invaders' and says he might send as many as 15,000 troops to counter what he views as a threat to the U.S.

Former Homeland Security chief Tom Ridge, a Republican, rebuffed Trump's claimed Thursday. He told VOA the '[term 'invasion' is very 'disproportionate' to any such threat.]

He said the call for more troops at the border is 'unnecessary rhetoric.' [A larger threat are opiods,] Ridge said. '[The real threats are terrorists that send pipe bombs to people and that assassinate on the Sabbath.]' "

– Reported by **VOA News** on October 31, 2018 regarding Trump at a Fort Meyers, Florida rally.

T-Brain's Two-Cents: Ahhh… Crazy is as crazy does. Trumpy, you crazy!

PRESS: Birthright citizenship. Are you going to sign an executive order to ban —

PRESIDENT: We are looking at it very seriously. Absolutely.

PRESS: I mean, is it yes or no? Or are you —

PRESIDENT: And I believe we have the absolute right. But that's another case that will be determined by the Supreme Court of the United States.

– **Trump on November 7, 2018 beginning at 11:57 AM EST in the East Room at the White House (Whitehouse.gov).**

T-Brain's Two-Cents: Not sure how else **Trumpy** could have answered that question! To answer it just one more time… ***Absolutely* looking into it!**

And don't dare us! We're ***STILL* thinking of doing it…**

PRESS: (Inaudible) sign an executive order on birthright citizenship this week. Why did that not happen?

PRESIDENT: We're working. Well, because other things have come up, and we will be signing it soon.

PRESS: Was it a political stunt?

PRESIDENT: No, no, no. Oh, we're signing it. We're doing it. And it'll probably work its way up to the Supreme Court. Birthright citizenship probably works its way up to the Supreme Court. It will be signed. We wanted a perfect document. And because of the election and all of the delays in the election, and whatever is going on in Broward County — remember the word, "Broward County."

– **Trump on the South Lawn beginning at 9:05 AM EST on November 9, 2018 (Whitehouse.gov).**

<u>Loco Thinking About Arming Schools & Places Of Worship?</u>

PRESIDENT: Why do we protect our airports, and our banks, our government buildings, but not our schools? (Applause.) It's time to make our schools a much harder target for attackers. We don't want them in our schools. (Applause.) We don't want them.

When we declare our schools to be gun-free zones, it just puts our students in far more danger. (Applause.) Far more danger. Well-trained, gun-adept teachers and coaches and people that work in those buildings; people that were in the Marines for 20 years and retired; people in the Army, the Navy, the Air Force, the Coast Guard; people that are adept — adept with weaponry and with guns — they teach. I mean, I don't want to have 100 guards standing with rifles all over the school. You do a concealed carry permit. (Applause.)

And this would be a major deterrent because these people are inherently cowards. If they thought — like, if this guy thought that other people would be shooting bullets back at him, he wouldn't have gone to that school. He wouldn't have gone there. It's a gun-free zone. It says, this is a gun-free zone; please check your guns way far away. And what happens is they feel safe. There's nobody going to come at them. ...

But as I've been talking about this idea — and I feel it's a great idea, but some people that are good people are opposed to it; they don't like the idea of teachers doing it. But I'm not talking about teachers. You know, CNN went on, they said, "Donald Trump wants all teachers." Okay? Fake news, folks. Fake news. Fake news.

I don't want a person that's never handled a gun that wouldn't know what a gun looks like to be armed. But out of your teaching population — out of your teaching population, you have 10 percent, 20 percent of very gun-adept people. Military people, law enforcement people, they teach. They teach. (Applause.) ...

But you know what I thought of as soon as I saw that? These teachers — and I've seen them at a lot of schools where they had problems — these teachers love their students. And the students love their teachers.

in many cases. These teachers love their students. And these teachers are talented with weaponry and with guns. And they feel safe. And I'd rather have somebody that loves their students and wants to protect their students than somebody standing outside that doesn't know anybody and doesn't know the students, and, frankly, for whatever reason, decided not to go in even though he heard lots of shots being fired inside. The teachers and the coaches and other people in the building — the dean, the assistant dean, the principal — they can — they love their people. They want to protect these kids. And I think we're better with that. And this may be 10 percent or 20 percent of the population of teachers, et cetera. It's not all of them. But you would have a lot, and you would tell people that they're inside. And the beauty is, it's concealed. Nobody would ever see it unless they needed it. It's concealed.

So this crazy man who walked in wouldn't even know who it is that has it. That's good. That's not bad; that's good. And a teacher would have shot the hell out of him before he knew what happened. (Applause.) They love their students. They love those students, folks. Remember that. They love their students.

And I'm telling you that would work. Because we need offensive capability. We can't just say, oh, it's a gun-free school. We're going to do it a little bit better. Because then you say, "What happens outside?" The students now leave school, and you got a thousand students — you got 3,500 at the school we're talking about — but you have a thousand students standing outside. The teachers are out there also. If a madman comes along, we have the same problem, but it's outside of the school. Or they drive cars. There are a lot of things that can happen.

–Trump at Conservative Political Action Conference in Gaylord National Resort & Convention Center in Maryland beginning at 10:16 AM EST on February 23, 2018 (Whitehouse.gov).

T-Brain's Two-Cents: Thaaaaat was a (loud)mouthful. He said it all!: www.whitehouse.gov/briefings-statements/remarks-president-trump-conservative-political-action-conference-2/

PRESS: That's what I'd like to follow up with you on. Do you think that all churches and synagogues should have armed guards?

PRESIDENT: I hate to think of it that way, I will say that. I hate to think of it that way. So we'll see you with the Future farmers.

PRESS: Is that what you're suggesting?

PRESIDENT: No, it's certainly an option. I mean, in this world — this is a world with a lot of problems. And it has been a world with a lot of problems for many years — many, many years, and you could say, frankly, for many centuries. I mean, you look at what goes on.

But certainly you want protection, and they didn't have any protection. They had a maniac walk in, and they didn't have any protection. And that is just so sad to see. So sad to see. The results could have been much better. It is a very, very — it's a very difficult thing. For me to stand as President and to watch any of this go — you know, before I ran for office, and I'd watch instances like this with churches and other things, I'd say, "What a shame. What a shame."

But it's even tougher when you're the President of the United States and you have to watch this kind of a thing happen. It is so sad to see. So we'll see you with the young farmers. A lot of them are out there.

PRESS: Do you think there's anything you can do with the NRA?

PRESIDENT: We're always talking. We're always talking.

—**Trump at Joint Base Andrews beginning at 12:34 P.M. EDT on October 27, 2018 (Whitehouse.gov).**

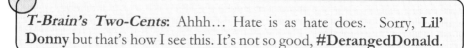

T-Brain's Two-Cents: Ahhh… Hate is as hate does. Sorry, **Lil' Donny** but that's how I see this. It's not so good, **#DerangedDonald**.

<u>Loco View Involving The Border?</u>

PRESIDENT: This is a national emergency.

PRESS: If it's a true national emergency, why haven't you declared a national emergency already?

PRESIDENT: Because I would like to do the deal through Congress, and because it makes sense to do it through Congress. But the easy route for me would have been call a national emergency and do it. And I will tell you, this is a tremendous crisis at the border. Look at President Obama's statements from the past. Numerous statements where he calls it a crisis. This is a crisis. You have human trafficking. You have drugs. You have criminals coming in. You have gangs, MS-13. We're taking them out by the thousand and bringing them back. This is a crisis. And they don't come in at the checkpoint, which they do also, but they go in between the checkpoints, where you don't have any barriers.

…

PRESS: So it's a national emergency. If this doesn't work out, you're (inaudible), but you will do it, or are you still thinking about it?

PRESIDENT: If we don't make a deal — I mean, I would say 100 percent, but I don't want to say 100 percent, because maybe something else comes up. But if we don't make a deal, I would say it would be very surprising to me that I would not declare a national emergency and just fund it through the various mechanisms. And, by the way, there's more than one mechanism. There's various mechanisms. And the lawyers tell me 100 percent. It would be nice if we could make a deal. But dealing with these people is ridiculous. I don't know if they know how to make a deal. It's — we need — and I'll tell you what: A lot of Democrats — I was looking at numbers — a lot of Democrats agree, Steve, we need national security. And the only way you have it — the only way you have it is you have to have a strong border. And the only way you have a strong border is you need a wall, or you need some kind of a steel — go ahead, Gardiner."

–**Trump on the South Lawn beginning at 9:32 AM EST on January 10, 2019 (Whitehouse.gov).**

T-Brain's Two-Cents: 100% loco talk since no bigly wall is going up.

41

E. Extreme Paranoia?

Paranoid About Former FBI Director James Comey?

"What is taking so long with the Inspector General's Report on Crooked Hillary and Slippery James Comey. Numerous delays. Hope Report is not being changed and made weaker! There are so many horrible things to tell, the public has the right to know. Transparency!"

(@realDonaldTrump)
June 5, 2018, 3:38 AM. Tweet

T-Brain's Two-Cents: Yes, **Trumpy** and I really don't care about this report. Even if it had come out on your birthday... we really just don't care...even though you clearly do care. Weak.

PRESS: Is the Comey report going to be your birthday present?

PRESIDENT: Well, it seems that it's coming out on my birthday. Maybe that's appropriate. Let's see if it is. Look, he's a very dishonest man; I've been saying it for a long time. I think I did our country a great fire – a really great favor when I fired him. And we'll see what happens. We'll see what the report says. But I guess it just got announced that it's coming out on June 14th, so that'll be maybe a nice birthday present. Who knows.

–Trump at South Lawn beginning at 8:02 A.M. EDT on June 8, 2018 (Whitehouse.gov).

President Trump claimed that former FBI Director James Comey and special counsel Robert Mueller are "best friends" and that he could provide 100 pictures showing them both "hugging and kissing."

– Trump in the Oval Office during an interview with *The Daily Caller* on September 5, 2018.

T-Brain's Two-Cents: Oof! Not sure what **Trumpy** was saying here but he sure did say it! Here's a summary of that interview. It's a **doozy!**

thehill.com/homenews/administration/405178-trump-i-could-show-you-100-photos-of-mueller-and-comey-hugging-and

The FBI stated that it could not find any pictures of FBI Director James Comey and special counsel Robert Mueller "hugging and kissing."

– In reference to an FBI statement on October 17, 2018 after they investigated certain of Trump's assertions from his *The Daily Caller* interview on September 5, 2018.

T-Brain's Two-Cents: Wait! What??! People took us seriously?! Come on! Lighten up, people! Anyway, yup… people sure did seem to take **Trumpy's** comments seriously. You can even check it out here:

thehill.com/blogs/blog-briefing-room/412796-fbi-unable-to-find-photos-of-comey-mueller-hugging-and-kissing-as

Paranoia For The Sake Of Paranoia?

"Just watched Wacky Tom Steyer, who I have not seen in action before, be interviewed by @jaketapper. He comes off as a crazed & stumbling lunatic who should be running out of money pretty soon. As bad as their field is, if he is running for President, the Dems will eat him alive!"

(@realDonaldTrump)
Oct 28, 2018, 10:03 AM. Tweet

(According to *Forbes*, hedge fund founder Thomas Steyer has an estimated net worth of $1.6 billion as of July 16, 2019.)

T-Brain's Two-Cents: I wonder how real that net worth estimate is for Steyer. Well, as long as that figure isn't based off of "**feelings**" then it should be more real than that of some of the whiny real estate owners and developers that are out there. Oops, **Trumpy**.

Paranoid During The Attorney General Jeff Sessions Era?

T-Brain's Two-Cents: Well… let's just say… he was awesome until he wasn't as awesome. You can even check out what **Trumpy** said…

"Attorney General Jeff Sessions has taken a VERY weak position on Hillary Clinton crimes (where are E-mails & DNC server) & Intel leakers!"

(@realDonaldTrump)
July 25, 2017, 3:12 AM. Tweet

"..This is a terrible situation and Attorney General Jeff Sessions should stop this Rigged Witch Hunt right now, before it continues to stain our country any further. Bob Mueller is totally conflicted, and his 17 Angry Democrats that are doing his dirty work are a disgrace to USA!"

(@realDonaldTrump)
Aug 1, 2018, 6:24 AM. Tweet

""Department of Justice will not be improperly influenced by political considerations." Jeff, this is GREAT, what everyone wants, so look into all of the corruption on the "other side" including deleted Emails, Comey lies & leaks, Mueller conflicts, McCabe, Strzok, Page, Ohr......"

(@realDonaldTrump)
Aug 24, 2018, 3:17 AM. Tweet

"....FISA abuse, Christopher Steele & his phony and corrupt Dossier, the Clinton Foundation, illegal surveillance of Trump Campaign, Russian collusion by Dems - and so much more. Open up the papers & documents without redaction? Come on Jeff, you can do it, the country is waiting!"

(@realDonaldTrump)
Aug 24, 2018, 3:28 AM. Tweet

"Jeff Sessions said he wouldn't allow politics to influence him only because he doesn't understand what is happening underneath his command position. Highly conflicted Bob Mueller and his gang of 17 Angry Dems are having a field day as real corruption goes untouched. No Collusion!"

(@realDonaldTrump)
Aug 25, 2018, 5:36 AM. Tweet

"Two long running, Obama era, investigations of two very popular Republican Congressmen were brought to a well publicized charge, just ahead of the Mid-Terms, by the Jeff Sessions Justice Department. Two easy wins now in doubt because there is not enough time. Good job Jeff......"

(@realDonaldTrump)
Sept 3, 2018, 11:25 AM. Tweet

"....The Democrats, none of whom voted for Jeff Sessions, must love him now. Same thing with Lyin' James Comey. The Dems all hated him, wanted him out, thought he was disgusting - UNTIL I FIRED HIM! Immediately he became a wonderful man, a saint like figure in fact. Really sick!"

(@realDonaldTrump)
Sept 3, 2018, 11:25 AM. Tweet

Then-current Sen. Jeff Flake (R-AZ) tweeted from @JeffFlake on **September 3, 2018** that he felt that the president's conduct was not one that was upholding the U.S. Constitution but was one that was instead looking to use the Department of Justice to 'settle political scores.'

T-Brain's Two-Cents: Woah! Easy, Jeff! It does look like you may have said all that and below is a deep-link to that tweet! Anyway, don't you remember President Reagan's **11th commandment... Though shalt not speak ill of any fellow Republicans**! (Of course, **Trumpy** can disregard that extra commandment or even all of them if he wants.)

twitter.com/JeffFlake/status/1036752487666122752

"U.S. Senator Ben Sasse, a member of the Senate Judiciary Committee, issued the following statement regarding the President's attack on the Department of Justice for indicting two Republican congressmen.

" 'The United States is not some banana republic with a two-tiered system of justice – one for the majority party and one for the minority party. These two men have been charged with crimes because of evidence, not because of who the President was when the investigations began. Instead of commenting on ongoing investigations and prosecutions, the job of the President of the United States is to defend the Constitution and protect the impartial administration of justice.' "

– Sen. Ben Sasse (R-NE) in a public statement released on September 3, 2018 on his congressional Website.

T-Brain's Two-Cents: Republicans!! Did you all forget about Reagan's 11th commandment?!? Anyway, Ben, I know you said the above and below is a link to it. It looks like that statement was titled **"Sasse: 'The United States Is Not Some Banana Republic.'**:

www.sasse.senate.gov/public/index.cfm/2018/9/sasse-the-united-states-is-not-some-banana-republic

"Republican lawmakers are joining opposition Democrats in criticizing President Donald Trump for remarks that many are interpreting as an assault on the country's judicial independence. he president criticized his attorney general earlier this week over charges his Justice Department brought against two Republican congressmen. New York Rep. Chris Collins was charged as part of an alleged insider-trading scheme. California Rep. Duncan Hunter is accused of misusing campaign funds. Both have pleaded not guilty.

"The president has long criticized his attorney general and the Justice Department over the ongoing probe into Russian election meddling by special counsel Robert Mueller. But the president's latest remarks have been denounced by legal experts and members of his own party for appearing to put political concerns ahead of criminal law.

"A spokesperson for House Speaker Paul Ryan told CNN that the Justice Department 'should [stay apolitical, and that Ryan takes seriously the charges against Collins and Hunter].'"

– As reported by *VOA News* on September 4, 2018 regarding comments from Republicans after Trump's remarks toward Attorney General Jeff Sessions earlier that week.

T-Brain's Two-Cents: It's about time! I guess there's still a liddle' bit of a spine in there somewhere for some of you.

"We are pleased to announce that Matthew G. Whitaker, Chief of Staff to Attorney General Jeff Sessions at the Department of Justice, will become our new Acting Attorney General of the United States. He will serve our Country well...."

(@realDonaldTrump)
Nov 7, 2018, 11:44 AM. Tweet

T-Brain's Two-Cents: **Trumpy** has always been a fast Tweet/twit typer! And he sure knows how to say **Thanks** *and* **Kinda No Thanks** all within 60 seconds! Check it out yourself!

"....We thank Attorney General Jeff Sessions for his service, and wish him well! A permanent replacement will be nominated at a later date."

(@realDonaldTrump)
Nov 7, 2018, 11:44 AM. Tweet

"Attorney General Jeff Sessions, in a resignation letter to Trump, said he was stepping down at the president's 'request,' suggesting he'd been pushed out of a job he'd refused to leave despite enduring a steady onslaught of presidential humiliations and insults over his recusal from the probe of Russian meddling in the 2016 presidential election."

– Reported by *VOA News* on on November 7, 2018 regarding AG Jeff Sessions and his resignation letter to White House chief of staff John Kelly.

T-Brain's Two-Cents: At least some are a liddle' more sincere, no?

"Attorney General Sessions is a leader of integrity who served our country well."

(@SenatorCollins)
Nov 7, 2018, 2:14 PM. Tweet

"It is imperative that the Administration not impede the Mueller investigation. I'm concerned Rod Rosenstein will no longer be overseeing the probe. Special Counsel Mueller must be allowed to complete his work without interference—regardless of who is AG."

(@SenatorCollins)
Nov 7, 2018, 2:14 PM. Tweet

Paranoid About Losing Elections?

"Elect more Republicans in November and we will pass the finest, fairest and most comprehensive Immigration Bills anywhere in the world. Right now we have the dumbest and the worst. Dems are doing nothing but Obstructing. Remember their motto, RESIST! Ours is PRODUCE!"

(@realDonaldTrump)
June 22, 2018, 4:00 AM. Tweet

T-Brain's Two-Cents: Yes!! "P" for **P**roduce or also **PARANOIA**!!

"At stake in this Election is whether we continue the extraordinary prosperity we have achieved - or whether we let the Radical Democrat Mob take a giant wrecking ball to our Country and our Economy! #JobsNotMobs"

(@realDonaldTrump)
Oct 22, 2018, 7:13 PM. Tweet

"#JOBSNOTMOBS! VOTE REPUBLICAN NOW!!"

(@realDonaldTrump)
Oct 31, 2018, 12:25 PM. Tweet

"Thank you Ohio! When you enter the voting booth tomorrow you will be making a simple choice. A vote for Republicans is a vote to continue our extraordinary prosperity. A vote for Dems is a vote to bring this Economic Boom crashing to a sudden, screeching halt. Vote @MikeDeWine!"

(@realDonaldTrump)
Nov 5, 2018, 1:26 PM. Tweet

"There is only one way to stop this Democrat-Led assault on our sovereignty – you have to VOTE Republican TOMORROW! Polling locations: http://Vote.GOP"

(@realDonaldTrump)
Nov 5, 2018, 5:05 PM. Tweet

T-Brain's Two-Cents: Yes, **Trumpy**!! We're #**KNOBS**NOTMOBS!

"Just out — in Arizona, SIGNATURES DON'T MATCH. Electoral corruption – Call for a new Election? We must protect our Democracy!"

**(@realDonaldTrump)
Nov 9, 2018, 12:33 PM. Tweet**

T-Brain's Two-Cents: Is this a case of… You pronounce it as "potato"… but he pronounces it as "potatoh." Who on earth is right?!?

Sen. Jeff Flake (R-AZ) tweeted on **November 9, 2018** at 7:46 PM that he disagreed with the president about any "electoral corruption" in AZ. Sen. Flake stated that there was no such evidence and that there were thousands of Arizonians that worked "in a non-partisan fashion" to make sure each vote was counted.

T-Brain's Two-Cents: Here's the deep-link to Jeff Flake 'brave' tweet:

twitter.com/JeffFlake/status/1061102769812226048

PRESS: Mr. President, the Democrats keep picking up more seats in the House, now more than 31 seats. Can you still describe (inaudible)?

PRESIDENT: It doesn't — whether they get a couple of more House seats, it doesn't matter. It doesn't matter. But you notice the votes never go the other way? They hire lawyers, and the votes don't ever seem to go the Republican way — although I hear —

PRESS: Do you have evidence of fraud?

PRESIDENT: Well, I don't know, you tell me. It's always the Democrats. It's always GPS Fusion. It's always crooked stuff.

PRESS: But there's no evidence that you have, is there?

PRESIDENT: Look — look at what happened. How many FBI are gone? How many Justice Department people are gone? That I found out — that I found out. There's a lot of bad stuff going on in this country, and we're finding out, and I'm getting to the bottom of it. And I've done a hell of a job. How many people have been fired from the FBI? You got Comey, you got McCabe, you got Strzok, you have Lisa Page, you have Baker. You have a whole list of people. There's a lot of crooked stuff going on.

But it is interesting; it always seems to go the way of the Democrats. Now, in Arizona, all of a sudden, out of the wilderness, they find a lot of votes. And she's — the other candidate is just winning by a hair. What's going on in a Florida is a disgrace. Go down and see what happened over the last period of time — 10 years. Take a look at Broward. Take a look at the total dishonesty of what happened with respect to Broward County. Broward County — just (inaudible) — Broward County/election. There's a lot of dishonesty.

…

PRESS: Is there any evidence of fraud in Broward County?

PRESIDENT: Wait. Well, you take a look at the past. Take a look at the past.

PRESS: Right now is there any?

PRESIDENT: And all of a sudden, they're finding votes? You mean after the election, they're finding votes? And then you look at her past, where she's already been convicted, and now they're finding votes. And you have this guy, Elias, who represented Hillary Clinton and a lot of very shady things. I think what you ought to do is get smart.

– **Trump on the South Lawn beginning at 9:05 AM EST on November 9, 2018 (Whitehouse.gov).**

T-Brain's Two-Cents: Hmm. I guess this reminds me about my next point of thought.. Mr. or Mrs. Reader, **Please Do Not Smoke Crack**.

Paranoia About Special Counsel's Investigation?

"The appointment of the Special Counsel is totally UNCONSTITUTIONAL! Despite that, we play the game because I, unlike the Democrats, have done nothing wrong!"

(@realDonaldTrump)
June 4, 2018, 7:01 AM. Tweet

"The inner workings of the Mueller investigation are a total mess. They have found no collusion and have gone absolutely nuts. They are screaming and shouting at people, horribly threatening them to come up with the answers they want. They are a disgrace to our Nation and don't..."

(@realDonaldTrump)
Nov 15, 2018, 4:14 AM. Tweet

"....care how many lives the ruin. These are Angry People, including the highly conflicted Bob Mueller, who worked for Obama for 8 years. They won't even look at all of the bad acts and crimes on the other side. A TOTAL WITCH HUNT LIKE NO OTHER IN AMERICAN HISTORY!"

(@realDonaldTrump)
Nov 15, 2018, 4:32 AM. Tweet

T-Brain's Two-Cents: ENOUGH WITH LARGE CAPS!! And if you keep it up with this paranoia talk about witches and collusion… well, you're just a poor poker player… *and* casino investor. Oops.

""Democrats can't find a Smocking Gun tying the Trump campaign to Russia after James Comey's testimony. No Smocking Gun...No Collusion." @FoxNews That's because there was NO COLLUSION. So now the Dems go to a simple private transaction, wrongly call it a campaign contribution,..."

(@realDonaldTrump)
Dec 10, 2018, 3:46 AM. Tweet

"....which it was not (but even if it was, it is only a CIVIL CASE, like Obama's - but it was done correctly by a lawyer and there would not even be a fine. Lawyer's liability if he made a mistake, not me). Cohen just trying to get his sentence reduced. WITCH HUNT!"

(@realDonaldTrump)
Dec 10, 2018, 4:00 AM. Tweet

"Rudy Giuliani, one of U.S. President Donald Trump's lawyers, is acknowledging that some officials with Trump's 2016 campaign may have colluded with Russia to help him win, but says that Trump himself did not. ...

"Giuliani's new concession about Trump campaign involvement with Moscow is sharply at odds with what Trump himself has tweeted at least 13 times, that his successful campaign for the White House did not collude with Russia, more recently last month.

"Russia has rejected the conclusion of the U.S. intelligence community that Moscow's agents meddled in the election to help Trump win, although President

Vladimir Putin acknowledged at last July's Helsinki summit with Trump that he wanted the then-real estate mogul to defeat his Democratic challenger, former U.S. Secretary of State Hillary Clinton. ...

"Giuliani's acknowledgement about Trump campaign ties to Russia came days after news surfaced, inadvertently, that Manafort shared campaign polling data with a former business associate of his in Ukraine alleged by U.S. prosecutors to have ties to Russian intelligence. ... Giuliani challenged Mueller to produce evidence of wrongdoing by Trump. ... Earlier this week, Trump, after news reports suggested he might be beholden to Russia and Putin, declared, 'I never worked for Russia' and told a reporter, 'I think it's a disgrace you even asked that question.'

"The New York Times reported last weekend that two years ago Federal Bureau of Investigation officials started investigating whether Trump 'was knowingly working for Russia or had unwittingly fallen under Moscow's influence' because of his behavior after he fired former FBI chief James Comey in May 2017 when he was leading the investigation into Russian meddling during the election."

– Reported by *VOA News* on January 17, 2019 regarding comments from Trump's attorney Rudy Giuliani.

T-Brain's Two-Cents: Say it ain't so, Rudy! **Trumpy** not gonna likey!

Paranoid About Presidential Eavesdropping?

"I'd bet a good lawyer could make a great case out of the fact that President Obama was tapping my phones in October, just prior to Election!"

(@realDonaldTrump)
March 4, 2017, 3:52 AM. Tweet

T-Brain's Two-Cents: I agree, **Trumpy**! But no **good lawyer** is going to take our case because you don't seem to bother to take good lawyers' advice! Argh!

CHAPTER THREE

VERY IMPAIRED THINKING?

"In my lifetime, I have made over 100,000 phone calls and maybe 1,000 of them are obscene! That's a very small percentage."

– Cam Brady in the comedy film *The Campaign*, 2012

T-Brain's Two-Cents: Cam Brady… you're a loser! Everyone knows it! And **Trumpy** could totally do much better than 1,000!

A. Very Easily Confused?

Confused About The Topic Of Climate?

"In most places, weather can change from minute to-minute, hour-to-hour, day-to-day, and season-to-season. Climate, however, is the average of weather over time and space. An easy way to remember the difference is that climate is what you expect, like a very hot summer, and weather is what you get, like a hot day with pop-up thunderstorms."

– National Aeronautics and Space Administration (NASA).

T-Brain's Two-Cents: Well, you can't say that NASA doesn't try to educate the public… like it is here. I just wish **Trumpy** could read this…and **read…this… slowly.** Here it is again on NASA's website:

www.nasa.gov/mission_pages/noaa-n/climate/climate_weather.html

"In the East, it could be the COLDEST New Year's Eve on record. Perhaps we could use a little bit of that good old Global Warming that our Country, but not other countries, was going to pay TRILLIONS OF DOLLARS to protect against. Bundle up!"

(@realDonaldTrump)
Dec 28, 2017, 4:01 PM. Tweet

"Brutal and Extended Cold Blast could shatter ALL RECORDS - Whatever happened to Global Warming?"

(@realDonaldTrump)
Nov 21, 2018, 4:23 PM. Tweet

T-Brain's Two-Cents: It just seems that ever since I began 'extracting' myself from his liddle' cranium... **Trumpy's** go-to responses are written in **ALL CAPS** or him saying "**I don't believe it**" or "**I don't care**." He seems to think that addresses things. Hmm.

"By 2090, days when it is too hot or too smoggy to work will cost the U.S. economy up to $155 billion each year in lost productivity. That's one economic impact cited in the National Climate Assessment released Friday by 13 U.S. federal agencies. 'Without substantial and sustained global mitigation and regional adaptation efforts, climate change is expected to cause growing losses to American infrastructure and property and impede the rate of economic growth over this century,' the report said. 'I don't believe it,' President Donald Trump responded when asked about the report Monday.

"Trump has for many years rejected the scientific consensus that human activities are the main drivers of climate change. Since his first day in office, he has worked to undo regulations that aim to cut the greenhouse gas emissions that are warming the planet. The focus has been on boosting the economy. According to the government's new report, failing to cut those emissions ultimately will take a significant toll on economic output."

– Reported by *VOA News* on November 26, 2018 and in regards Trump's four-word response about a National Climate Assessment report.

Confused About U.S. Postal System And A Guy Named Bezos?

"Amazon is doing great damage to tax paying retailers. Towns, cities and states throughout the U.S. are being hurt - many jobs being lost!"

(@realDonaldTrump)
Aug 16, 2017, 3:12 AM. Tweet

"Why is the United States Post Office, which is losing many billions of dollars a year, while charging Amazon and others so little to deliver their packages, making Amazon richer and the Post Office dumber and poorer? Should be charging MUCH MORE!"

(@realDonaldTrump)
Dec 29, 2017, 5:04 AM. Tweet

"I have stated my concerns with Amazon long before the Election. Unlike others, they pay little or no taxes to state & local governments, use our Postal System as their Delivery Boy (causing tremendous loss to the U.S.), and are putting many thousands of retailers out of business!"

(@realDonaldTrump)
March 29, 2018, 4:57 AM. Tweet

T-Brain's Two-Cents: Bro, you gotta relax. People can see through this. I think you just don't like **The Bezos** because he – unlike many, many and MANY (*wink wink*) others – grew his net worth bigly and it's now **well over $100 billion**. And Bezos also jumped **higher** (actually, he jumped to the top spot *instead of falling by 11 spots*) on the Forbes 400 (2018) list. (Ouch, **Mr. Just-A-Single-Digit-Billionaire!**)

"For years, Trump has been at odds with Amazon founder and CEO Jeff Bezos, who owns the Washington Post newspaper. ... "Online news site Axios cited five unnamed sources in a report Wednesday that said Trump wants to [pursue] Amazon... According to the Axios report... It quotes another source saying, [on multiple occasions people have explained that the post office actually generates considerable amounts of money from Amazon]. Amazon, founded in 1994, is the world's largest Internet retailer measured by revenue and market capitalization. Last year, with over 40 subsidiaries, the company's revenue exceeded $177 billion."

– Reported by *VOA News* on March 29, 2018 about news site *Axios'* report on Trump and his thoughts about Amazon and its founder Jeff Bezos.

T-Brain's Two-Cents: **Trumpy**, what's going on? Well... could just be a case of... L.O.S.T. C.A.U.S.E. That's how you spell it. And, **Trumpy**, below is how you show it? Or maybe it's just semantics.

"While we are on the subject, it is reported that the U.S. Post Office will lose $1.50 on average for each package it delivers for Amazon. That amounts to Billions of Dollars. The Failing N.Y. Times reports that "the size of the company's lobbying staff has ballooned," and that..."

(@realDonaldTrump)
March 31, 2018, 5:45 AM. Tweet

"...does not include the Fake Washington Post, which is used as a "lobbyist" and should so REGISTER. If the P.O. "increased its parcel rates, Amazon's shipping costs would rise by $2.6 Billion." This Post Office scam must stop. Amazon must pay real costs (and taxes) now!"

(@realDonaldTrump)
March 31, 2018, 5:52 AM. Tweet

Confused With Question About Problem With Women Voters?

PRESS: Aixa Diaz with Hearst Television. You've said, "Pretend I'm on the ballot" — yesterday. You called it a referendum on your presidency. Many local districts across the country rejected your midterm message, particularly suburban women. How do you bridge that divide now — also with the influx of women coming into Congress?

PRESIDENT: I think my message was very well received. I mean, just look at the results. Midterm elections are disasters for sitting Presidents and administrations. This has been a very successful — and, look, you can write it any way you want. And if you disagree with me — this has been incredibly success — when you look at the races. How about Ohio? I didn't even mention. I mentioned Florida; I mentioned Georgia. How about the governor of Ohio? A fantastic —

PRESS: But what's your message to suburban women voters?

PRESIDENT: Excuse me. Excuse me. Excuse me. A fantastic man, who was down on the polls. And everybody was talking about this person that was so great. And I went up there, and I did a rally, and they have now a great governor — you're going to have a great governor in Ohio for, hopefully, a long period of time. But for four years. And — Mike DeWine is a fantastic person.

And I went up there for two reasons: Because I felt that his opposition was not a good person — and we know a lot about him — and I felt that Mike was a fantastic person. And he won. And not only did he win, he won easily.

So add that to Florida, and add that to Georgia, and add that to all of the other races that we won — outside, even, of the Senate races, which were the biggest of all. Because these were races that — and Mike Pence can tell you, and some of the folks over here can tell you — these were races that were going to be unopposed. We were not going to oppose certain of the people running — certain senators. They said they couldn't be beaten. They said Heidi could not be beaten. "Please, don't do it." This was a year out.

PRESS: What about in the suburban districts? How do you get those back?

PRESIDENT: Excuse me. You — no, but you're telling me about — you're telling me about popularity. They said many of these people — when I said 9 out of 11 — but I said — when many of these people — these weren't like easy races; they were tough races.

And so I think the level of popularity — the first question I was asked was about, "Well, what have you learned? What about your own popularity?" I think that's what I learned, is — I was very well received by this great country, by the people of our great country. And I'm very proud of that, because I love the people of this country. These people — we are the greatest people. I love the people of our country.

PRESS: So what do you say to women, Mr. President?

PRESIDENT: And I'll tell you something: When you look at the races that we won in Florida, which we weren't expected to win; and Georgia, which we weren't expected to win; and Ohio, which we weren't expected to win — and won; I mean, you look at some of them — the number of votes that we got is incredible. So I'm really happy with not only the way it came out, but the response to me as your President. And as your President, I made our country safe. I've rebuilt and am in the process of rebuilding our military. And the jobs are here.

Every one of them built here. We're going to have the strongest — very shortly, we're going to have the strongest military our country has ever had.

I've done more for the vets than any President has done, certainly in many, many decades, with Choice and with other things, as you know. With other things.

– Trump at the White House on November 7, 2018 following the results of the 2018 midterm elections (Whitehouse.gov).

T-Brain's Two-Cents: Soooooooooooo, **Trumpy**... Just one more time and just to be very very clear... What's your answer again to the question of what you'd say to women? (You, freakin' liddle' douche.)

B. Very Jumbled Speech?

A Beauty Of A Jumbled Jamboree Speech?

PRESIDENT: Tonight, we put aside all of the policy fights in Washington, D.C. -- you've been hearing about with the fake news and all of that. (Applause.) We're going to put that aside. And instead we're going to talk about success, about how all of you amazing young Scouts can achieve your dreams. What to think of -- what I've been thinking about -- you want to achieve your dreams. I said, who the hell wants to speak about politics when I'm in front of the Boy Scouts? Right? (Applause.) …

You know, I go to Washington and I see all these politicians, and I see the swamp. And it's not a good place. In fact today I said we ought to change it from the word swamp to the word cesspool or, perhaps, to the word sewer. But it's not good. Not good. (Applause.) And I see what's going on, and believe me I'd much rather be with you. That I can tell you. (Applause.) …

Secretary Tom Price is also here. Today Dr. Price still lives the Scout Oath, helping to keep millions of Americans strong and healthy as our Secretary of Health and Human Services. And he's doing a great job. And hopefully, he's going to get the votes tomorrow to start our path toward killing this horrible thing known as Obamacare that's really hurting us, folks. (Applause.)

AUDIENCE: USA! USA! USA!

PRESIDENT: By the way, you going to get the votes?

He better get them. He better get them. Oh, he better – otherwise, I'll say, Tom, you're fired. I'll get somebody. (Applause.)

He better get Senator Capito to vote for it. You got to get the other senators to vote for it. It's time. After seven years of saying repeal and replace Obamacare, we have a chance to now do it. They better do it. Hopefully they'll do it. ...

I'm waving to people back there so small I can't even see them. Man, this is a lot of people. Turn those cameras back there, please. That is so incredible.

By the way, what do you think the chances are that this incredible, massive crowd, record-setting is going to be shown on television tonight? One percent or zero? (Applause.)

The fake media will say: President Trump – and you know what this is – President Trump spoke before a small crowd of Boy Scouts today. That's some – that is some crowd. (Applause.)

Fake media. Fake news. Thank you. And I'm honored by that, by the way, all of you people they can't even see you. So thank you. I hope you can hear. And by the way, under the Trump administration, you'll be saying, merry Christmas again when you go shopping. Believe me. Merry Christmas. (Applause.) They've been downplaying that little, beautiful phrase. You're going to be saying, merry Christmas again, folks. (Applause.)

– Trump at the 2017 National Scout Jamboree held by the Boy Scouts of America beginning at 6:32 PM EDT on July 24, 2017 in Summit Bechtel Reserve, West Virginia (Whitehouse.gov *originally***).**

T-Brain's Two-Cents: Yup. This kinda actually happened. The leader of the Free World opened his mouth aaaaaaaand...... all that came out! Even the White House originally posted this, likely then had second thoughts and then eventually removed it...but no worries!! Here's a link to that original transcript since the Internet archives everything... And there's more to it than what see you above. **Yikes!**

web.archive.org/web/20170725150204/https://www.whitehous e.gov/the-press-office/2017/07/24/remarks-president-trump-2017-national-scout-jamboree

Jumbled To Purposefully Confuse?

PRESIDENT: There was no collusion at all. And people have seen that, and they've seen that strongly. The House has already come out very strongly on that. A lot of people have come out strongly on that.

I thought that I made myself very clear by having just reviewed the transcript. Now, I have to say, I came back, and I said, "What is going on? What's the big deal?" So I got a transcript. I reviewed it. I actually went out and reviewed a clip of an answer that I gave, and I realized that there is need for some clarification.

It should have been obvious — I thought it would be obvious — but I would like to clarify, just in case it wasn't. In a key sentence in my remarks, I said the word "would" instead of "wouldn't." The sentence should have been: I don't see any reason why I wouldn't — or why it wouldn't be Russia. So just to repeat it, I said the word "would" instead of "wouldn't." And the sentence should have been — and I thought it would be maybe a little bit unclear on the transcript or unclear on the actual video — the sentence should have been: I don't see any reason why it wouldn't be Russia. Sort of a double negative.

So you can put that in, and I think that probably clarifies things pretty good by itself. I have, on numerous occasions, noted our intelligence findings that Russians attempted to interfere in our elections. Unlike previous administrations, my administration has and will continue to move aggressively to repeal any efforts — and repel — we will stop it, we will repel it — any efforts to interfere in our elections. We're doing everything in our power to prevent Russian interference in 2018.

– Trump in the Roosevelt Room at White House beginning at 2:22 PM EDT on July 17, 2018 (Whitehouse.gov).

T-Brain's Two-Cents: WTF, people! Obviously, when **Trumpy** said "would" he meant "wouldn't" but only when he meant for you to read it as "wouldn't" otherwise it would just be "would" if that makes sense which it does because it's obvious if it wasn't already strongly clear.

<u>Jumbled Into Make-Believe?</u>

PRESIDENT: We're cracking down on sanctuary cities. Can you believe this? (Applause.) Where they protect — that's another one. Because we want our cities to be sanctuaries for law-abiding Americans, not for criminals. (Applause.)

And, by the way, the Senate Democrats and the House Democrats have totally abandoned DACA. They've total — they don't even talk to me about it. They have totally abandoned. You know, we get the reputation — like DACA, it's not Republican. We'll let me tell you, it is Republican, because we want to do something about DACA, get it solved after all these years.

The Democrats are being totally unresponsive. They don't want to do anything about DACA, I'm telling you. And it's very possible that DACA won't happen, and it's not because of the Republicans, it's going to be because of the Democrats. And frankly, you better elect more Republicans, folks, or it will never happen. (Applause.)

– Trump at the Conservative Political Action Conference held at the Gaylord National Resort and Convention Center in Oxon Hill, Maryland on February 23, 2018 (Whitehouse.gov).

T-Brain's Two-Cents: Ahhh… I'll be honest with you, **Trumpy**… I'm not even sure I followed **WTF** you were trying to say here since some of what you said doesn't make sense or simply add up. Of course, if you were just trying to spread pixie dust….then **A+**!

'Jumbled' Preparation?

PRESS: Were you serious about really not needing to prepare for the Kim summit? Or were you –

PRESIDENT: No, I didn't say that. I said I've been preparing all my life. I always believe in preparation, but I've been preparing all my life. You know, these one-week preparations, they don't work. Just ask Hillary what happened to her in the debates.

So I've been preparing for this all my life. And frankly, it's really just the fake news. Because if you run, Peter, just a little but longer, the clip, you would see: I've really been preparing all my life. I said that, but, you know, the news doesn't pick that up because it's fake news.

– Trump at the South Lawn beginning at 8:02 A.M. EDT on June 8, 2018 (Whitehouse.gov).

T-Brain's Two-Cents: Well, **Trumpy,** I think that Fake News did previously pick up on you insinuating that you've **prepared for stuff like this all your life…** **BUT** I don't think they took you that seriously about that. Of course, now they know you're really really really serious.

'Jumbled' Frenemy?

PRESS: Before the meeting with President Putin, you called him an adversary, a rival, and yet you expressed hope that you would be able to bring this relationship to a new level. Did you manage to do this?

PRESIDENT: Actually, I called him a competitor. And a good competitor he is. And I think the word "competitor" is a – it's a compliment. I think that we will be competing, when you talk about the pipeline. I'm not sure necessarily that it's in the best interest of Germany or not, but that was a decision that they made. We'll be competing – as you know, the United States is now, or soon will be – but I think it actually is right now – the largest in the oil and gas world.

So we're going to be selling LNG and we'll have to be competing with the pipeline. And I think we'll compete successfully, although there is a little advantage locationally. So I just wish them luck. I mean, I did. I discussed with Angela Merkel in pretty strong tones. But I also know where they're all coming from. And they have a very close source. So we'll see how that all works out.

But we have lots of sources now, and the United States is much different than it was a number of years ago when we weren't able to extract what we can extract today. So today we're number one in the world at that. And I think we'll be out there competing very strongly.

Thank you very much.

– Trump at a joint press conference with Russian President Putin in Helsinki, Finland on July 16, 2018 (Whitehouse.gov).

T-Brain's Two-Cents: Not sure what else to add here other than: #GoodCompetitorHeIs #NumberOneAtThat #VeryStrongly. (Oh and because I don't think he knows what's right for the U.S.: **#Loser**).

Please Don't Call Me... Mr. Jumbles?

In a public interview, Trump explained in two sentences the distinction between bad laws and good laws.

– Trump at the White House in an interview with *Fox & Friends* host Ainsley Earhardt on August 22, 2018 (aired August 23, 2018).

T-Brain's Two-Cents: Wow.. another beauty. And one can easily find this quote all over the Internet by just **googling** in a single search these words altogether and as shown with the quotation marks:

trump know "bad laws" good but "good laws" better

PRESS: But you say you were against chain migration. And the First Lady said that you and she both agreed family members should be allowed in.

PRESIDENT: Chain migration is not a good thing. Chain migration is bad. If you take a look at the lottery system, that's bad. What I want is merit. I want a lot of people to come in. We have great car companies entering our country again. This hasn't happened for 35 years. We have companies like Foxconn going to Wisconsin with a massive, massive plant.

We need people coming in, but we want them to come in on a merit. We want people that are going to help us. It's very important. We want them to come in on a merit basis.

– **Trump at the South Lawn beginning at 3:52 P.M. EDT on October 13, 2018 (Whitehouse.gov).**

T-Brain's Two-Cents: Of course, merit is very very very important to **Trumpy**. You think of the word '**merit**' and, of course, most people think… President **Trumpy**. (Or as I call him… Mr. D**emerit**.)

Jumbled Into A Beauty Of A Long Incoherent Sentence?

All within 98-seconds, presidential candidate Donald Trump covered a myriad of topics that included good genes, Wharton School of Finance, MIT, an uncle, nuclear deal, building a fortune, credentials, being disadvantaged, women being smarter, the power, four (and previously three) prisoners, Persian negotiators and Iranians.

– Trump at the Magnolia Hall of the Sun City Hilton Head in Bluffton (Sun City), South Carolina on July 21, 2015.

T-Brain's Two-Cents: You can easily find online videos of this public speech that includes the above which is a seemingly **295-word single sentence**. It is **so worth** the time and effort to find it and to then watch/hear this **oh-so rambling sentence**. When **googling**, use in a single search these words altogether and without quotation marks:

trump campaign south carolina july 21 2015

And if you come across a copy of the complete video of this approximately 45-minute public speech then just **go straight to about minute 34:40. Enjoy!**

C. Very Out Of Touch With Reality?

Out Of Touch With Voter Fraud?

"The Fox News interview also included a question about Trump's call for investigating voter fraud in the November presidential election. Trump has made many claims that undocumented immigrants voting illegally cost him the national popular vote. Trump won the Electoral College vote to defeat Democratic challenger Hillary Clinton, but he lost the popular vote by nearly three million votes. '[I'll have you know… When 'illegals' are seen on the 'registration rolls'],' Trump said. '[There are 'illegals,' people that are dead, that is what you have. The situation is not good, it is quite bad.]'

"Election officials who have analyzed the November 8 vote say there were almost no indications of voter fraud, certainly not on the scale Trump cites."

– Reported by *VOA News* on February 6, 2017 about Trump in a February 3, 2017 interview with *Fox News* host Bill O'Reilly

T-Brain's Two-Cents: Hey, **Mikey Pence**!! Where are you?! **Trumpy** and I asked you to look into **voter fraud**! Status update please? Seriously… if you can't produce results for a task you were assigned to lead then… well, I guess, go back to staring at the nearest wall when your boss speaks.

Out Of Touch With Prohibitions On Military Cooperation?

PRESS: Excuse me, but, for now, no specific agreements? For instance, between the militaries?

PRESIDENT: Well, our militaries do get along. In fact, our militaries, actually, have gotten along probably better than our political leaders for years. But our militaries do get along very well, and they do coordinate in Syria and other places.

– Trump at a joint press conference with Russian President Putin in Helsinki, Finland on July 16, 2018 (Whitehouse.gov).

T-Brain's Two-Cents: This is a **brain-stumper** and well... I'm a brain! I'd just say: **#WTF**. Trumpy needs to listen to smart(**er**) people.

"The commander of U.S. forces in the Middle East says he has not received new guidance from the Pentagon on military cooperation with Russia in Syria following the Helsinki summit between President Donald Trump and Russian President Vladimir Putin. 'We have received no specific direction at this point,' U.S. Army General Joseph Votel, who leads U.S. Central Command, told reporters at the Pentagon via teleconference from Tampa, Florida, Thursday.

"Votel added that his forces are continuing communications to deconflict operations with the Russian military in Syria in order to 'ensure protection' of U.S. forces. ...

"General Votel reiterated on Thursday that U.S. law, adopted following Russia's annexation of Crimea, prohibits bilateral cooperation with the Russian military. Exceptions 'would have to be created by Congress or a waiver,' he said.

– Reported by *VOA News* on July 19, 2018 and includes comments from U.S. Army General Joseph Votel, four-star general in the U.S. Army and commander of United States Central Command, made from Tampa, FL.

Out Of Touch With Grocery Shopping?

President Trump stated at a rally that stricter laws on voter ID were necessary and that one already needs a picture ID to buy groceries.

– Trump at rally in Tampa, Florida on July 31, 2018 (*The Hill*).

T-Brain's Two-Cents: Way to go, **Trumpy**!! Let them have it! Yup, **Trumpy** sure did say that. Of course, on the flip side… This is one of many public instances of him being so out of touch! And you can follow or enter this link to read more about what he said at that rally about grocery shopping from this *The Hill* article dated **July 31, 2018**:

thehill.com/homenews/administration/399806-trump-falsely-claims-id-is-required-to-buy-groceries

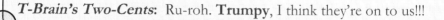

T-Brain's Two-Cents: Ru-roh. **Trumpy**, I think they're on to us!!!

PRESS: When was the last time the President went to a grocery store?

MS. SANDERS: I'm not sure. I'm not sure why that matters, either. Major, go ahead.

PRESS: Well, because of what he said last night. Because he said you need an —

PRESS: He said last night that you need an ID to buy —

PRESS: You go to the grocery store; I go to a grocery store. I've never had to show an ID to buy my groceries.

MS. SANDERS: I've been a lot lately, actually.

PRESS: I've never had to show an ID when I go to buy groceries. Most people don't.

MS. SANDERS: Certainly if you go to a grocery store and you buy beer and wine, you're certainly going to show your ID. I don't think that —

PRESS: Is that what the President, who doesn't drink, meant?

MS. SANDERS: He's not saying every time he went in. He said when "you" go to the grocery story. I'm pretty sure that everybody in here who's been to a grocery store and has purchased beer or wine has probably had to show their ID. If they didn't, then that's probably a problem with the grocery store.

– **Press Secretary Sarah Sanders at the James S. Brady Press Briefing Room beginning at 1:32 PM EDT on August 1, 2018 (Whitehouse.gov).**

78

'Out Of Touch' Whacko?

T-Brain's Two-Cents: **Trumpy**, why did you use the word "whako." It'll give people ideas about other whackos. Uhhh… Ahem.

PRESIDENT: But it looks like the results are coming in and they're far more devastating than anybody originally thought in the morning. In the morning, they thought that it was a shooter but they had the shooter, or they soon would. But the results are very devastating. You're seeing the numbers come in.

So we'll be speaking to you at the conference, the Future Farmers of America Conference. And it's just a shame to watch this and to see this. For so many years, so much of it is absolutely a shame.

Do you have any questions?

PRESS: Mr. President, do you think you need to revisit gun laws?

PRESIDENT: I can't – talk up a little bit.

PRESS: Gun laws.

PRESS: Gun laws.

PRESIDENT: Well, again, this has little to do with it if you take a look. If they had protection inside, the results would have been far better. This is a dispute that will always exist, I suspect. But if they had some kind of a protection inside the temple, maybe it could have been a very much different situation, but they didn't. And he was able to do things that, unfortunately, he shouldn't have been able to do.

…

PRESS: Mr. President, do you think there's anything you can do – you said it happens again and again – to end this kind of violence?

PRESIDENT: Well, it's a violence that's – you look at the violence all over the world. I mean, the world has violence. The world is a violent world. And you think when you're over it, it just sort of goes away, but then it comes back in the form of a mad man, a whacko. I think one thing we should is we should stiffen up our laws in terms of the death penalty. When people do this, they should get the death penalty, and they shouldn't have to wait years and years.

– Trump at Joint Base Andrews in Maryland beginning at 12:34 P.M. EDT on October 27, 2018 after reports that day of the fatal shootings at the Tree of Life synagogue in Pittsburgh, Pennsylvania (Whitehouse.gov).

Out Of Touch With Nature?

T-Brain's Two-Cents: **Trumpy**, I'll let you take over with just this liddle' section on **Nature**. You do an excellent job (**A+!**) covering both sides of…whatever **gobbledygook** you're trying to say here.

"Today on Earth Day, we celebrate our beautiful forests, lakes and land. We stand committed to preserving the natural beauty of our nation."

(@realDonaldTrump)
April 22, 2017, 12:01 PM. Tweet

"There is no reason for these massive, deadly and costly forest fires in California except that forest management is so poor. Billions of dollars are given each year, with so many lives lost, all because of gross mismanagement of the forests. Remedy now, or no more Fed payments!"

(@realDonaldTrump)
Nov 10, 2018, 12:08 AM. Tweet

"With proper Forest Management, we can stop the devastation constantly going on in California. Get Smart!"
Nov 11, 2018, 1:40 AM. Tweet

"More than 4,000 are fighting the Camp and Woolsey Fires in California that have burned over 170,000 acres. Our hearts are with those fighting the fires, the 52,000 who have evacuated, and the families of the 11 who have died. The destruction is catastrophic. God Bless them all."

(@realDonaldTrump)
Nov 10, 2018, 2:19 PM. Tweet

"These California fires are expanding very, very quickly (in some cases 80-100 acres a minute). If people don't evacuate quickly, they risk being overtaken by the fire. Please listen to evacuation orders from State and local officials!"

(@realDonaldTrump)
Nov 10, 2018, 2:20 PM. Tweet

"Billions of dollars are sent to the State of California for Forest fires that, with proper Forest Management, would never happen. Unless they get their act together, which is unlikely, I have ordered FEMA to send no more money. It is a disgraceful situation in lives & money!"

(@realDonaldTrump)
Jan 9, 2019, 7:25 AM. Tweet

An Out-Of-Touch-With-How-Business-Works Businessman?

PRESS: (Inaudible) talk to Mary Barra at General Motors?

PRESIDENT: I did. I spoke to her and I expressed the fact that I am not happy with what she did. You know, the United States saved General Motors, and for her to take that company out of Ohio is not good. I think she's going to put something back in soon. That car is not selling. It's a Cruze — Chevy Cruze. It's not selling.

But hopefully, she's going to come back and she's going to put something. But I told her I'm not happy about it at all.

PRESS: (Inaudible.)

PRESIDENT: No, not tariffs. It had nothing to do with tariffs. She said the car was not selling.

– Trump at the South Lawn beginning at 2:44 P.M. EST on November 26, 2018 (Whitehouse.gov).

T-Brain's Two-Cents: Let me see if I can sum this up… **'You, bad. Me, smart. You, not good. Me, not happy.'** Ha! How was that?

D. Very Much Making Things Up?

Just…Making…Things….Up?

"The W.H. is functioning perfectly, focused on HealthCare, Tax Cuts/Reform & many other things. I have very little time for watching T.V."

(@realDonaldTrump)
July 12, 2017, 6:39 AM. Tweet

T-Brain's Two-Cents: Little time for TV? **Trumpy**, that's funny AND adorable. You silly guy you and… you #LiddleDummy.

"Many Gang Members and some very bad people are mixed into the Caravan heading to our Southern Border. Please go back, you will not be admitted into the United States unless you go through the legal process. This is an invasion of our Country and our Military is waiting for you!"

(@realDonaldTrump)
Oct 29, 2018, 7:41 AM. Tweet

T-Brain's Two-Cents: What?! **Invasion?!** Come on, Trumpster. You know better. You're just making crap up. Enough with this silliness.

PRESS: Mr. President, what happens to the children then? If you're ending catch-and-release, what happens to those children? Do they stay in these tent cities? Or what happens?

PRESIDENT: We're working on a system where they stay together. But I will say that, by doing that, tremendous numbers — you know, under the Obama plan, you could separate children. They never did anything about that. Nobody talks about that. But under President Obama, they separated children from the parents. We actually put it so that that didn't happen.

But what happens when you do that is you get tremendous numbers of people coming. It's almost like an incentive to — when they hear they're not going to be separated, they come many, many times over. But President Obama separated the children, the parents. And nobody complained. When we continued the exact same law, this country went crazy.

– Trump in the Roosevelt Room at the White House beginning at 4:19 PM EDT on November 1, 2018 (Whitehouse.gov).

T-Brain's Two-Cents: Alright... enough is enough, **Douche**. You're being self-serving. And you're just being a dick, **Dick**. And when I say dick... I mean tiny, **Tiny**. – Love, T-Brain, a **Liddle' Brain**

PRESS: Are you prepared to fly that flag at half-mast a lot more?

PRESIDENT: Well, I don't like abusing any privilege, but when I see something that we should do, I always do that. Yeah, I always do that. I believe you should. When somebody — when it's a worthy situation, I do believe it.

– Trump on the South Lawn beginning at 9:05 AM EST on November 9, 2018 (Whitehouse.gov).

PRESS: Mr. President, the latest research from NOAA says that climate change will make the strongest hurricanes even stronger. Do you agree with that assessment?

PRESIDENT: I'll have to look at it. I haven't seen that. But I would certainly have to look at it.

PRESS: When you see impacts like this to the U.S., does it affect at all your decision in renegotiating the Paris Climate Accord?

PRESIDENT: No, I want crystal clean water. I want the cleanest air on the planet — which, by the way, now we have. It's gotten better since last year — even better. And I'm very, very tough on that.

So when you talk about environmental, I am truly an environmentalist. A lot people smile when they hear that. But I have the cleanest air, and I'm going to have the cleanest air. But that doesn't mean we have to put every one of our businesses out of business. That doesn't mean that we can't compete or we're not allowed to compete with other nations that aren't doing what we're doing.

And we're competing very well. Our nation is the hottest nation economically on the planet, by far, even though we're very big. I mean, we're up $10.7 [trillion] — $11.7 trillion, since I got elected. Nobody thought that would be possible. And other nations — as an example, China — not that I wish this, but they're down many trillions of dollars. So we're doing really well, and I want to keep it that way.

– **Trump at Georgia Operations Center for the Red Cross in Macon, Georgia on October 15, 2018 in the aftermath of Hurricane Michael (Whitehouse.gov).**

T-Brain's Two-Cents: Hmmm… where to begin. '**Tone deaf**' doesn't seem to be enough of a descriptor. '**Uncaring**' doesn't quiet cut it either. **#DerangedDonald** is certainly a goodie but not for the above. So, maybe I'll just run with something like… **Donny Douche**.

E. Very Easily Irritable?

All In A Day's Most 'Irritable' Work?

T-Brain's Two-Cents: Sometimes I wonder if it is never too old to act like a **7-year old liddle' lyin' brat?**... Never. Proceed, **Trumpy**:

"Bob Corker, who helped President O give us the bad Iran Deal & couldn't get elected dog catcher in Tennessee, is now fighting Tax Cuts...."

(@realDonaldTrump)
Oct 24, 2017, 5:13 AM. Tweet

"...Corker dropped out of the race in Tennesse when I refused to endorse him, and now is only negative on anything Trump. Look at his record!"

(@realDonaldTrump)
Oct 24, 2017, 5:20 AM. Tweet

"Same untruths from an utterly untruthful president. #AlertTheDaycareStaff"

(@SenBobCorker)
Oct 24, 2017, 5:48 AM. Tweet

"Isn't it sad that lightweight Senator Bob Corker, who couldn't get re-elected in the Great State of Tennessee, will now fight Tax Cuts plus!"

> **(@realDonaldTrump)**
> **Oct 24, 2017, 6:30 AM. Tweet**

"Sen. Corker is the incompetent head of the Foreign Relations Committee, & look how poorly the U.S. has done. He doesn't have a clue as....."

> **(@realDonaldTrump)**
> **Oct 24, 2017, 7:13 AM. Tweet**

"...the entire World WAS laughing and taking advantage of us. People like liddle' Bob Corker have set the U.S. way back. Now we move forward!"

> **(@realDonaldTrump)**
> **Oct 24, 2017, 7:20 AM. Tweet**

Really Just Most 'Irritated' At Two People?

"The reason Flake and Corker dropped out of the Senate race is very simple, they had zero chance of being elected. Now act so hurt & wounded!"

> **(@realDonaldTrump)**
> **Oct 25, 2017, 4:27 AM. Tweet**

T-Brain's Two-Cents: Sometimes me wonders… Is it really never too old to *act like an*… **annoying liddle' seven-year old brat?** Nope. Never. Especially when you're **The Trumpet**. Check for yourself:

"The meeting with Republican Senators yesterday, outside of Flake and Corker, was a love fest with standing ovations and great ideas for USA!"

(@realDonaldTrump)
Oct 25, 2017, 4:30 AM. Tweet

"Working hard on the biggest tax cut in U.S. history. Great support from so many sides. Big winners will be the middle class, business & JOBS"

(@realDonaldTrump)
Oct 25, 2017, 4:35 AM. Tweet

"Jeff Flake, with an 18% approval rating in Arizona, said "a lot of my colleagues have spoken out." Really, they just gave me a standing O!"

(@realDonaldTrump)
Oct 25, 2017, 5:33 AM. Tweet

"Trump said media reports of his feuds with figures across the U.S. political spectrum make 'me more uncivil than I am. You know, people don't understand. I went to an Ivy League college. I was a nice student. I did very well. I'm a very intelligent person. I, you know, the fact is I think — I really believe, I think the press creates a different image of Donald Trump than the real, the real person.'

"Trump's rebuke of Flake and Corker came a day after both lawmakers had offered brutal commentary on the first nine months of his presidency.

"Flake, in a speech on the Senate floor, announced he would not seek another six-year term in the November 2018 elections, then slammed Trump's behavior as 'dangerous to our democracy' and called on other Republicans to denounce the president's conduct. 'It is time for our complicity and our accommodation of the unacceptable to end,' Flake said. 'Politics can make us silent when we should speak, and silence can equal complicity.'

"He added, 'We must never regard as normal the regular and casual undermining of our democratic norms and ideals. We must never meekly accept the daily sundering of our country — the personal attacks; the threats against principles, freedoms and institutions; the flagrant disregard for truth and decency.' His speech came after Corker and Trump traded taunts for hours.

"[Corker:] 'Standing up in front of the American people and stating untruths that everybody knows to be untrue, attempted bullying that he does, which everybody sees through, just the dividing of our country, the name-callings, for young people to be watching, not only here in our country but around the world, someone of this mentality as president of the United States is something that is I think debasing to our country,' Corker said. 'You would think he would aspire to be the president of the United States and act like a president of the United States.'

"[Corker:] 'But that's just not going to be the case, apparently,' he concluded.

– Reported by *VOA News* on October 25, 2017 and in regards to comments from Trump as he spoke to the press about his rebukes of Sen. Bob Corker (R-TN) and Sen. Jeff Flake (R-AZ) – both of whom are also quoted here as speaking critically about Trump from Capitol Hill.

T-Brain's Two-Cents: Well, **Trumpy**… You know, I had told you to lay off on some of these pointed attacks in your periodic nonsensical **Tweetacks**… and so no wonder **#DerangedDonald** is taking quite a run! Argh!!

CHAPTER FOUR

EXTREME ANXIOUSNESS?

"She's become seriously unhinged. She has gone full-metal Nixon."

– Amy Brookheimer referring to U.S. President Selina Meyer in *HBO's* political satire comedy series *Veep* (Season 5, Episode 6: C**tgate – May 29, 2016) .

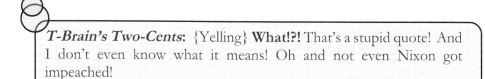

T-Brain's Two-Cents: {Yelling} **What!?!** That's a stupid quote! And I don't even know what it means! Oh and not even Nixon got impeached!

A. Impending Panic?

So 'Panicky' About One Lady?

"The First Lady [Hillary Clinton] is a wonderful woman who has handled pressure incredibly well."

– Donald J. Trump in *Trump: The Art of The Comeback* (1997)

T-Brain's Two-Cents: Ahhh… **Oopsie!** I think they're on to us again, **Trumpy**! Yup, I double checked, Trumpmeister. You did say the above on **page xix**. Argh. I guess that was before the **#DonnyDouche** era. Oh well.

"Crooked Hillary Clinton is the worst (and biggest) loser of all time. She just can't stop, which is so good for the Republican Party. Hillary, get on with your life and give it another try in three years!"

(@realDonaldTrump)
Nov 18, 2017, 5:31 AM. Tweet

Is This On-Setting Panic Self-Inflicted?

"Importantly, I recused myself not because of any asserted wrongdoing on my part during the campaign, but because a Department of Justice regulation, 28 CFR 45.2, required it. That regulation states, in effect, that Department employees should not participate in investigations of a campaign if they have served as a campaign advisor."

— **Attorney General Jeff Sessions speaking to the Senate Intelligence Committee on June 13, 2017 (DoJ).**

T-Brain's Two-Cents: Hey, **Mr. Magoo**, it's a simple rule: If **Trumpy** says it's **Fake NEWS** then you must **NOT RECUSE**! But as T-Brain I'm also torn cause if you take Russian gloves & **Trumpy's stubby** fingers slide right in… If they **FIT** you must **NOT ACQUIT!**

"The Russian Witch Hunt Hoax continues, all because Jeff Sessions didn't tell me he was going to recuse himself...I would have quickly picked someone else. So much time and money wasted, so many lives ruined...and Sessions knew better than most that there was No Collusion!"

(@realDonaldTrump)
June 5, 2018, 4:31 AM. Tweet

"U.S. President Donald Trump unleashed a new broadside against Attorney General Jeff Sessions on Tuesday [June 5, 2018], blaming him for the year-long investigation into Trump's 2016 campaign links to Russia because he removed himself from oversight of the probe.

"More than a year ago, Sessions recused himself from oversight of what eventually became special counsel Robert Mueller's investigation of Russian meddling in the election and whether Trump obstructed justice by firing FBI director James Comey when he was leading the probe. Days after Comey's ouster, Sessions' deputy attorney general, Rod Rosenstein, over Trump's objections, named Mueller to take over the investigation.

"Sessions, while he was a senator from Alabama, was the first major Washington political figure to support Trump's long shot presidential bid that ended with him winning a four-year term in the White House. But after Trump named Sessions as attorney general, the government's top legal official, Sessions adhered to long-standing Justice Department rules prohibiting lawyers from involvement in investigations in which they have a conflict of interest.

"Sessions had two conflicts: He was a vocal Trump supporter and had met twice with Russia's ambassador to Washington during the campaign. Trump has often berated Sessions, calling him 'weak' and 'beleaguered,' and has unsuccessfully sought to get him to reverse his decision to remove himself from oversight of the Mueller investigation. But the president has not fired Sessions, warned by key Republican senators that they had no intention of confirming any new selection Trump might make for attorney general if Sessions were dismissed."

— Reported by *VOA News* on June 5, 2018 and includes comments from Trump regarding Attorney General Jeff Sessions.

T-Brain's Two-Cents: Well, me thinks Trumpy was going light when he called Jeffy just **beleaguered** and **weak**. He should be grateful.

'Panicky' About Relations With Russia?

PRESS: Thank you. Mr. President, you tweeted this morning that it's U.S. foolishness, stupidity, and the Mueller probe that is responsible for the decline in U.S. relations with Russia. Do you hold Russia at all accountable for anything in particular? And if so, what would you consider them – that they are responsible for?

PRESIDENT: Yes, I do. I hold both countries responsible. I think that the United States has been foolish. I think we've all been foolish. We should have had this dialogue a long time ago – a long time, frankly, before I got to office. And I think we're all to blame. I think that the United States now has stepped forward, along with Russia. And we're getting together. And we have a chance to do some great things, whether it's nuclear proliferation, in terms of stopping – because we have to do it. Ultimately, that's probably the most important thing that we can be working on.

But I do feel that we have both made some mistakes. I think that the probe is a disaster for our country. I think it's kept us apart. It's kept us separated. There was no collusion at all. Everybody knows it. People are being brought out to the fore.

So far, that I know, virtually none of it related to the campaign. And they're going to have try really hard to find somebody that did relate to the campaign. That was a clean campaign. I beat Hillary Clinton easily. And frankly, we beat her – and I'm not even saying from the standpoint – we won that race. And it's a shame that there can even be a little bit of a cloud over it. People know that. People understand it. But the main thing, and we discussed this also, is zero collusion. And it has had a negative impact upon the relationship of the two largest nuclear powers in the world. We have 90 percent of nuclear power between the two countries. It's ridiculous. It's ridiculous what's going on with the probe.

— **Trump at a joint press conference with Russian President Putin in Helsinki, Finland on July 16, 2018 (Whitehouse.gov).**

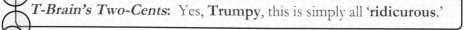

T-Brain's Two-Cents: Yes, **Trumpy**, this is simply all '**ridicurous.**'

PRESS: Thank you. A question for each President. President Trump, you first. Just now, President Putin denied having anything to do with the election interference in 2016. Every U.S. intelligence agency has concluded that Russia did. What — who — my first question for you, sir, is, who do you believe?

My second question is, would you now, with the whole world watching, tell President Putin — would you denounce what happened in 2016? And would you warn him to never do it again?

PRESIDENT: So let me just say that we have two thoughts. You have groups that are wondering why the FBI never took the server. Why haven't they taken the server? Why was the FBI told to leave the office of the Democratic National Committee? I've been wondering that. I've been asking that for months and months, and I've been tweeting it out and calling it out on social media. Where is the server? I want to know, where is the server? And what is the server saying?

With that being said, all I can do is ask the question. My people came to me — Dan Coats came to me and some others — they said they think it's Russia. I have President Putin; he just said it's not Russia.

I will say this: I don't see any reason why it would be, but I really do want to see the server. But I have — I have confidence in both parties. I really believe that this will probably go on for a while, but I don't think it can go on without finding out what happened to the server. What happened to the servers of the Pakistani gentleman that worked on the DNC? Where are those servers? They're missing. Where are they? What happened to Hillary Clinton's emails? Thirty-three thousand emails gone — just gone. I think, in Russia, they wouldn't be gone so easily. I think it's a disgrace that we can't get Hillary Clinton's 33,000 emails.

So I have great confidence in my intelligence people, but I will tell you that President Putin was extremely strong and powerful in his denial today. And what he did is an incredible offer; he offered to have the people working on the case come and work with their investigators with respect to the 12 people. I think that's an incredible offer.

Trump at a joint press conference with Russian President Putin in Helsinki, Finland on July 16, 2018 (Whitehouse.gov).

Panic Over Others Hurting Michael Cohen, A 'Fine Person'?

"The New York Times and a third rate reporter named Maggie Haberman, known as a Crooked H flunkie who I don't speak to and have nothing to do with, are going out of their way to destroy Michael Cohen and his relationship with me in the hope that he will "flip." They use...."

(@realDonaldTrump)
April 21, 2018, 6:10 AM. Tweet

"....non-existent "sources" and a drunk/drugged up loser who hates Michael, a fine person with a wonderful family. Michael is a businessman for his own account/lawyer who I have always liked & respected. Most people will flip if the Government lets them out of trouble, even if...."

(@realDonaldTrump)
April 21, 2018, 6:10 AM. Tweet

"....it means lying or making up stories. Sorry, I don't see Michael doing that despite the horrible Witch Hunt and the dishonest media!"

(@realDonaldTrump)
April 21, 2018, 6:10 AM. Tweet

T-Brain's Two-Cents: Yes, just as **Trumpy** has said, Mr. Cohen has been **always liked & respected** and is **a fine person with a wonderful family.**

"Inconceivable that the government would break into a lawyer's office (early in the morning) - almost unheard of. Even more inconceivable that a lawyer would tape a client - totally unheard of & perhaps illegal. The good news is that your favorite President did nothing wrong!"

(@realDonaldTrump)
July 21, 2018, 5:10 AM. Tweet

T-Brain's Two-Cents: Wait… what?! Mike taped our conversations?!

T-Brain's Two-Cents: Mikey, why?! WHY!?! No matter. Hey, people, your **favorite President** is A – Okay.

"What kind of a lawyer would tape a client? So sad! Is this a first, never heard of it before? Why was the tape so abruptly terminated (cut) while I was presumably saying positive things? I hear there are other clients and many reporters that are taped - can this be so? Too bad!"

(@realDonaldTrump)
July 25, 2018, 5:34 AM. Tweet

"If anyone is looking for a good lawyer, I would strongly suggest that you don't retain the services of Michael Cohen!"

(@realDonaldTrump)
Aug 22, 2018, 5:44 AM. Tweet

"Michael Cohen plead guilty to two counts of campaign finance violations that are not a crime. President Obama had a big campaign finance violation and it was easily settled!"

(@realDonaldTrump)
Aug 22, 2018, 6:37 AM. Tweet

T-Brain's Two-Cents: Trumpy… #DONENOTHINGWRONG

PRESS: Thank you, Sarah. Michael Cohen, under oath, pleaded guilty to — among things — paying Stormy Daniels and Karen McDougal during the campaign. And he says he did it at the direction of the President of the United States. Did President Trump commit a crime?

SANDERS: As the President said, and we've stated many times, he did nothing wrong. There are no charges against him. And we've commented on this extensively.

PRESS: Then why not report these payments?

SANDERS: Again, I'm not going to get into the back-and-forth details. I can tell you, as the President has stated on numerous occasions, he did nothing wrong. There are no charges against him in this. And just because Michael Cohen made a plea deal doesn't mean that that implicates the President on anything.

…

PRESS: Sarah, does the President feel betrayed by Michael Cohen? And is he concerned about what he might say to Robert Mueller?

SANDERS: I don't think the President is concerned at all. He knows that he did nothing wrong and that there was no collusion. And we're going to continue focusing on the things that Americans care about and that we can have an impact on.

– Press Secretary Sarah Sanders in the James S. Brady Press Briefing Room beginning at 2:26 PM EDT on August 22, 2018 (Whitehouse.gov).

""Michael Cohen asks judge for no Prison Time." You mean he can do all of the TERRIBLE, unrelated to Trump, things having to do with fraud, big loans, Taxis, etc., and not serve a long prison term? He makes up stories to get a GREAT & ALREADY reduced deal for himself, and get....."

(@realDonaldTrump)
Dec. 3, 2018, 7:24 AM. Tweet

T-Brain's Two-Cents: Yes, just as **Trumpy** has said, Mr. Cohen has been ~~always liked & respected~~ and ~~is~~ a ~~fine~~ person with a ~~wonderful~~ family.

"....his wife and father-in-law (who has the money?) off Scott Free. He lied for this outcome and should, in my opinion, serve a full and complete sentence."

(@realDonaldTrump)
Dec. 3, 2018, 7:29 AM. Tweet

38 minutes after the above tweet from the president, a dictionary tweeted the definitions of 'Scot-free' and 'Scott Free.'

– @MerriamWebster sent its tweet on December 3, 2018 at 8:07 AM. This tweet can be found by googling the following words altogether without quotations and in a single search:

merriam thinks scott free is probably some guy

T-Brain's Two-Cents: I guess if it's not "**Scott Free**" then it can't be "**Scotty Free**" either. Well, the **dictionary** was awoken and it tweeted. And it was a **beauty of a tweet**. You can also find that tweet here:
twitter.com/MerriamWebster/status/1069624230701092864

"I never directed Michael Cohen to break the law. He was a lawyer and he is supposed to know the law. It is called "advice of counsel," and a lawyer has great liability if a mistake is made. That is why they get paid. Despite that many campaign finance lawyers have strongly......"

(@realDonaldTrump)
December 13, 2018, 5:17 AM. Tweet

"....stated that I did nothing wrong with respect to campaign finance laws, if they even apply, because this was not campaign finance. Cohen was guilty on many charges unrelated to me, but he plead to two campaign charges which were not criminal and of which he probably was not..."

(@realDonaldTrump)
December 13, 2018, 5:25 AM. Tweet

"....guilty even on a civil basis. Those charges were just agreed to by him in order to embarrass the president and get a much reduced prison sentence, which he did-including the fact that his family was temporarily let off the hook. As a lawyer, Michael has great liability to me!"

(@realDonaldTrump)
December 13, 2018, 5:39 AM. Tweet

***T-Brain's Two-Cents*:** Come on, people! As these many long and early morning tweets show, **Trumpy** clearly doesn't care about any of this and nor is he concerned whatsoever about all of this about Cohen.

"Remember, Michael Cohen only became a "Rat" after the FBI did something which was absolutely unthinkable & unheard of until the Witch Hunt was illegally started. They BROKE INTO AN ATTORNEY'S OFFICE! Why didn't they break into the DNC to get the Server, or Crooked's office?"

(@realDonaldTrump)
December 16, 2018, 6:39 AM. Tweet

Panic Over Others Hurting Paul Manafort, A Loyal Friend?

"I feel very badly for Paul Manafort and his wonderful family. "Justice" took a 12 year old tax case, among other things, applied tremendous pressure on him and, unlike Michael Cohen, he refused to "break" - make up stories in order to get a "deal." Such respect for a brave man!"

(@realDonaldTrump)
Aug 22, 2018, 6:21 AM. Tweet

"A large number of counts, ten, could not even be decided in the Paul Manafort case. Witch Hunt!"

(@realDonaldTrump)
Aug 22, 2018, 6:34 AM. Tweet

T-Brain's Two-Cents: That's right, **Trumpy**. And people need to realize that as Trumpy and I see it… Manafort had nothing to do with **Trumpy**, nothing do with his campaign and nothing to do with the White House. Sarah, please take it from here…

PRESS: Is the President now planning on, or intent on, pardoning Paul Manafort?

SANDERS: The Manafort case doesn't have anything to do with the President, doesn't have anything to do with his campaign, and it doesn't have anything to do with the White House.

...

PRESS: Sarah, in his tweet about Paul Manafort this morning, the President seemed to be praising him for essentially refusing to cooperate with federal prosecutors in a way that could implicate him, the President. Is that what he meant to suggest? And doesn't that seem to indicate that he thinks that loyalty to him personally is more important with abiding by the law or cooperating with this government in an investigation?

SANDERS: Not at all. The Manafort case doesn't involve the President, doesn't involve his campaign, and has nothing to do with the White House. The President has expressed his views.

– Press Secretary Sarah Sanders in the James S. Brady Press Briefing Room beginning at 2:26 PM EDT on August 22, 2018 (Whitehouse.gov).

B. Feeling Extreme Hopelessness?

Hopelessly Without A Partisan U.S. Attorney General?

"U.S. President Donald Trump launched an array of attacks Wednesday [September 19, 2018] on Attorney General Jeff Sessions, disparaging Sessions' performance as the country's top law enforcement official. 'I'm disappointed in the attorney general for many reasons,' Trump told reporters at the White House. His remark came hours after a television interview with HillTV aired in which Trump declared [that he did not think he had an attorney general and that that was quite sad].

"Trump for more than a year has railed against Sessions, the first senator to declare his support for then-candidate Trump in 2016. Trump continues to vent his anger at Sessions for removing himself from oversight of the long-running investigation of Russia links to Trump's campaign and whether, as president, Trump obstructed justice by trying to thwart the probe.

"Sessions has said that he was required by Justice Department dictates to recuse himself from overseeing the probe because he staunchly backed Trump's campaign and also had two contacts in 2016, when he was a senator from Alabama, with Russia's then-ambassador to Washington. Oversight of the Russia probe then fell to Deputy Attorney General Rod Rosenstein, who in turn, over Trump's objections, appointed Robert Mueller, a former director of the Federal Bureau of Investigation, as special counsel to head the investigation.

– Reported by *VOA News* on September 19, 2018 and includes comments from Trump during and after an interview he had with *Hill.TV* in the Oval Office.

T-Brain's Two-Cents: It's hard not to think... **Trumpy** just wanted his AG to do his bidding. Is that so wrong? He hired him after all, no?

Hopelessly Without Partisan U.S. Federal Judges?

"Whatever the scope of the President's authority, he may not rewrite the immigration laws to impose a condition that Congress has expressly forbidden. Defendants' claims that the rule can somehow be harmonized with the [Immigration and Naturalization Act] are not persuasive.

"Also, Plaintiffs and the immigrants they represent will suffer irreparable injury if the rule goes into effect pending resolution of this case. Asylum seekers will be put at increased risk of violence and other harms at the border, and many will be deprived of meritorious asylum claims. The government offers nothing in support of the new rule that outweighs the need to avoid these harms."

– U.S. District Judge Jon S. Tigar of the United States District Court for the Northern District of California in a ruling against the government ("Defendant") that was signed on November 19, 2018 (SCOTUS).

T-Brain's Two-Cents: Oof! This is a bit of a doozy for **Trumpy**. At first (orange) blush, this ruling kinda made sense and seemed nonpartisan-ish, but **Tantrump** viewed it differently and this certainly set him off!! You can find the full ruling and this filing at the Websites of either this federal court or the American Civil Liberties Union.

"Well, you go the 9th Circuit and it's a disgrace. And I'm going to put in a major complaint because you cannot win – if you're us – a case in the 9th Circuit and I think it's a disgrace. ... This was an Obama judge. And I'll tell you what, it's not going to happen like this anymore."

– Trump comments on the South Lawn beginning at 3:11 P.M. EST on November 20, 2018 (Whitehouse.gov). This was in response to the federal court issuing a temporary restraining order on November 19, 2018 against the president's attempt to refuse asylum to immigrants who arrive between ports of entry.

"U.S. President Donald Trump started his Thanksgiving holiday by renewing his public debate over the independence of the country's judicial system. In a teleconference Thursday [November 22, 2018] with American troops overseas, Trump said a federal appeals court in California has become 'a big thorn in our side.'

"The president's remarks came one day after he and U.S. Chief Justice John Roberts engaged in an extraordinary exchange over the independence of the federal judiciary, with Roberts admonishing Trump for criticizing a judge who ruled against his administration as an 'Obama judge.'

Roberts, appointed by Republican President George W. Bush, responded with a rare public rebuke of the president, saying Trump's comments reflect his misunderstanding of the judiciary's role. 'We do not have Obama judges or Trump judges, Bush judges or Clinton judges,' Roberts said in a bluntly worded statement [on November 21, 2018]. 'What we have is an extraordinary group of dedicated judges doing their level best to do equal right to those appearing before them. That independent judiciary is something we should all be thankful for.'

"Although it is very unusual for a president to personally criticize judges, Trump quickly responded by questioning the independence of federal judges appointed by his predecessor and confirmed by the Senate."

– Reported by *VOA News* on November 22, 2018 and includes remarks by Trump made during a call with American troops.

T-Brain's Two-Cents: Some may think this is all **smoke and mirrors**. Nope! It's just **your favorite president** taking a (childish) stand! Bravo, **Liddle' Donny!**

"Sorry Chief Justice John Roberts, but you do indeed have "Obama judges," and they have a much different point of view than the people who are charged with the safety of our country. It would be great if the 9th Circuit was indeed an "independent judiciary," but if it is why......"

(@realDonaldTrump)
Nov 21, 2018, 12:51 PM. Tweet

".....are so many opposing view (on Border and Safety) cases filed there, and why are a vast number of those cases overturned. Please study the numbers, they are shocking. We need protection and security - these rulings are making our country unsafe! Very dangerous and unwise!

(@realDonaldTrump)
Nov 21, 2018, 1:09 PM. Tweet

"Justice Roberts can say what he wants, but the 9th Circuit is a complete & total disaster. It is out of control, has a horrible reputation, is overturned more than any Circuit in the Country, 79%, & is used to get an almost guaranteed result. Judges must not Legislate Security..."

(@realDonaldTrump)
Nov 22, 2018, 4:21 AM. Tweet

"....and Safety at the Border, or anywhere else. They know nothing about it and are making our Country unsafe. Our great Law Enforcement professionals MUST BE ALLOWED TO DO THEIR JOB! If not there will be only bedlam, chaos, injury and death. We want the Constitution as written!"

(@realDonaldTrump)
Nov 22, 2018, 4:30 AM. Tweet

C. Difficulty Concentrating?

Concentrating On Not Drawing Instead The Russian Flag?

T-Brain's Two-Cents: **RussianFlagGate** never got traction… but whether he really knew what he was doing or not… It sure seemed like he was coloring in a Russian flag! Hey, **Trumpy**… **#BeMoreSubtle**:

www.theguardian.com/us-news/shortcuts/2018/aug/27/trump-new-american-flag-russian-twist-us-president-drawing-children-ohio

PRESS: Will you recognize Russia's annex — will you recognize Crimea as part of Russia when you meet President —

PRESIDENT: Oh, that's an interesting question — because long before I got here, President Obama allowed that to happen. That was on his watch, not on my watch. You know, people like to say, "Oh, Crimea." But the fact is, they built bridges to Crimea. They just opened a big bridge that was started years ago. They built, I think, a submarine port; substantially added billions of dollars. So that was on Barack Obama's watch. That was not on Trump's watch. Would I have allowed it to happen? No, I would not have allowed it to happen. But he did allow it to happen, so that was his determination.

What will happen with Crimea from this point on? That I can't tell you. But I'm not happy about Crimea. But again, that was on Barack Obama's watch, not Trump's watch.

– Trump after NATO Summit in Brussels, Belgium beginning at 12:21 PM CEST on July 12, 2018 (Whitehouse.gov).

T-Brain's Two-Cents: **Trumpy**, you really need to **#ManUp**. And you should fix things if you think they're broken, **#LiddleDouche**.

Trouble Concentrating On Not Saying, 'Yes, I Will Pardon'?

PRESS: Thanks a lot, Sarah. Since those guilty verdicts yesterday in the Paul Manafort trial, the President has said some kind things about Mr. Manafort. He's called him a "good man," a "good person." He said he feels badly for what has happened to him. He tweeted today, "…unlike Michael Cohen, he refused to 'break' — make up stories in order to get a 'deal.'" He tweeted, "Such respect for a brave man!" Is Mr. Manafort a simple candidate for a presidential pardon?

SANDERS: Once again, that's not something that has been up for discussion. I don't have anything for you on that.

– Press Secretary Sarah Sanders in the James S. Brady Press Briefing Room beginning at 2:26 PM EDT on August 22, 2018 (Whitehouse.gov).

T-Brain's Two-Cents: Well, let's see: Pardons me, Pardons me **NOT**, Pardons me, Pardons me **NOT**, Pardons me… Damn it. Just do whatever you want at this point, **Mr. One-Termer**. (Oopsie!)

"U.S. President Donald Trump said Wednesday [November 28, 2018] that a pardon for his onetime 2016 campaign chairman, Paul Manafort, who is facing years in prison for financial fraud, was 'not off the table.' Trump told the New York Post in a White House interview that he had never discussed pardoning the 69-year-old longtime lobbyist. 'But I wouldn't take it off the table,' Trump said. 'Why would I take it off the table?'

"In August, a jury in northern Virginia, just outside Washington, found Manafort guilty of eight counts of tax and bank fraud stemming from his work as a political consultant in Ukraine that predated six months of work, including three as chairman, on Trump's successful 2016 run for the White House.

"Manafort later pleaded guilty in Washington to two new counts — conspiracy against the U.S., which involved financial crimes, and conspiracy to obstruct justice — and agreed to cooperate with special counsel Robert Mueller's investigation of possible Trump campaign links to Russia and whether Trump, as president, obstructed justice to try to thwart the probe. ...

"Trump claimed in the interview with the New York tabloid that Mueller had asked Manafort, former Trump political adviser Roger Stone and Stone's associate, Jerome Corsi, to lie about their roles in the 2016 political campaign in order to implicate others in the Trump orbit. 'If you told the truth, you go to jail,' Trump said of the prosecutors' pressure on witnesses. 'You know, this flipping stuff is terrible,' Trump said of witnesses asked to implicate higher-ups. 'You flip and you lie and you get — the prosecutors will tell you 99 percent of the time they can get people to flip. It's rare that they can't.' ... 'It's actually very brave,' Trump said of Manafort, Stone and Corsi. 'But this is where we are. And it's a terrible thing.'"

– Reported by *VOA News* on November 28, 2018 and includes Trump in the Oval Office during a *New York Post* interview

***T-Brain's Two-Cents*: Trumpy**, I'll take it from here. In summary:

Flipping = Terrible
Telling Truth = Jail Time
So When You Flip = You Lie
Since Getting 'Em To Flip = Easy To Do
Therefore, Not Flipping = Actually Very Brave

Of course, this all makes sense (in **Bizarro World**).

Slow Down Please… One Thing At A Time?

PRESIDENT: So we're heading off to Europe. It should be a very beautiful period of time — the 100th anniversary of the ending of World War I. We have many countries; the leadership of many countries will be there, especially since they heard the United States will be there. And we look forward to that. It'll be a great, really, commemorative service. I think it's going to be something very special. I've seen what they have planned, and I think it's going to be something very, very special.

I just signed the proclamation on asylum. Very important. People can come in, but they have to come in through the ports of entry. And that, to me, is a very important thing. Again, I reiterate we needs Democrats' votes. They have to pass new immigration laws, because they're flooding our country. We're not letting them in, but they're trying to flood our country. We need the wall; we're building the wall. But we need it all built at one time, and quickly. It's very important.

We need Democrat support on new immigration laws to bring us up to date. The laws are obsolete and they're incompetent. They are the worst laws any country has anywhere in the world. And it's only because we don't have the Democrats' votes. So we need Democrat vote so we can change immigration, and we'll have no trouble whatsoever at the border. We want people to come into our country, but they have to come into our country legally. They have to come into our country legally.

– **Trump on the South Lawn beginning at 9:05 AM EST on November 9, 2018 (Whitehouse.gov).**

T-Brain's Two-Cents: **Trumpmunch**, you so lack focus… which is why you won't get much done on immigration and your "wall."

D. You Sound Nervous?

So A 'Not-Nervous-At-All-Because-Of-NO-Collusion' Vibe?

PRESS: Mr. President, if Robert Mueller asks you to come and speak with his committee personally, are you committed, still, to doing that? Do you believe that's appropriate for a President?

PRESIDENT: Yeah. Just so you understand — just so you understand, there's been no collusion; there's been no crime. And in theory, everybody tells me I'm not under investigation. Maybe Hillary is, I don't know, but I'm not.

But there's been no collusion. There's been no crime. But we have been very open. We could have done it two ways. We could have been very closed and it would have taken years. But you know, it's sort of like, when you've done nothing wrong, let's be open and get it over with.

Because, honestly, it's very, very bad for our country. It's making our country look foolish, and this is a country that I don't want looking foolish. And it's not going to look foolish as long as I'm here. So we've been very open and we just want to get that over with.

– **Trump after the Congressional Republican Leadership Retreat at Camp David in Hauvers, Maryland beginning at 12:00 PM EST on January 6, 2018 (Whitehouse.gov).**

T-Brain's Two-Cents: **Trumpy,** just remind them one more time… **No collusion, no crime!** (But it might actually help more if you just *stopped* talking about it, **Trumpy.** You clearly can't though even at your own retreat! Sad.)

113

PRESS: You're finishing up the written answers —

PRESIDENT: What?

PRESS: You're doing the written questions to Robert Mueller. Have you ruled out a sit-down, an in-person sit-down with Robert Mueller?

PRESIDENT: I haven't ruled out anything. I haven't even thought about it. I'm thinking about the world. Right now, I'm thinking about the world. I'm not thinking about sit-downs or not sit-downs. There was no collusion. It's a whole hoax. This was a thing set up by the Democrats, just like they set up other things — when you look at what's going on Florida; when you look at what's going on in lots of different locations.

The Russian investigation is a hoax. It's a phony hoax. I didn't speak to Russians. The fact is, I was a much better candidate than Hillary Clinton. I worked much harder. I went to the right places. She went to the wrong places, because she didn't know what the hell she was doing. I did a great job; I was a great candidate. She was a bad candidate.

– **Trump on the South Lawn and beginning at 9:05 AM EST on November 9, 2018 (Whitehouse.gov).**

T-Brain's Two-Cents: Fine, **Mr. One-Termer**, just remind them here one more time... **A hoax, a whole hoax, a phony hoax!**

So… You're Saying You Don't Know Who Julian Assange Is?

(Note: Australian Julian Assange helped found WikiLeaks in 2006.)

President Trump remarked in an interview that WikiLeaks was 'disgraceful' and that their actions deserved the 'death penalty' for publishing classified U.S. documents and videos that were leaked to the organization and that were related to Pfc. Chelsea Manning, known at the time as Pfc. Bradley Manning.

- Trump in an interview with *Fox News* anchor Brian Kilmeade on December 2, 2010.

T-Brain's Two-Cents: **Trumpy**, not sure how to explain this one away about you referring to Assange's WikiLeaks. I guess if readers want to read even more about it…

thehill.com/homenews/campaign/312679-trump-in-2010-wanted-death-penalty-for-wikileaks

President Trump praised WikiLeaks and told an audience that he loved WikiLeaks. This occurred days after WikiLeaks's released on October 7, 2016 the hacked emails of Hillary Clinton.

- Trump at a campaign rally in Wilkes-Barre, Pennsylvania on October 10, 2016

T-Brain's Two-Cents: **Trumpy**… Ah… it's getting a liddle' harder to NOT show that you don't know anything about Assange-meister:

thehill.com/blogs/ballot-box/presidential-races/300327-trump-i-love-wikileaks

Prior to his inauguration and in early January 2017, Mr. Trump tweeted multiple times in reference to Julian Assange.

- Trump tweeted once on January 4, 2017 at 4:22 AM and twice on January 5, 2017 at 5:25 AM and 5:45 AM about Julian Assange.

T-Brain's Two-Cents: Yikes! Well, it's kinda hard at this point to NOT admit that you know who this **douche** is. Isn't that right, **Trumpy**? Here's how readers can find these 3 pre-presidency tweets:

- **1st tweet**: Googling these words/numbers once in a single search: assange trump twitter 2017 "4:22"

  or follow/enter this link:
  twitter.com/realDonaldTrump/status/816620855958601730

- **2nd tweet**: Googling these words/numbers once in a single search: assange trump twitter 2017 "5:25"

  or follow/enter this link:
  twitter.com/realDonaldTrump/status/816999062562107392

- **3rd tweet**: Googling these words/numbers once in a single search: intelligence trump twitter 2017 "5:45"

  or follow/enter this link:
  twitter.com/realDonaldTrump/status/980063581592047617

PRESS: Do you think Julian Assange should go free? (Inaudible.)

PRESIDENT: I don't know anything about him. Really, I don't know much about him. I really don't.

–Trump on the South Lawn beginning at 3:11 P.M. EST on November 20, 2018 (Whitehouse.gov).

Nervous About One Of The Lowest Inaugural Attendances?

PRESIDENT: And I was explaining about the numbers. We did a thing yesterday at the speech [The Inaugural Address]. Did everybody like the speech? (Applause.) I've been given good reviews. But we had a massive field of people. You saw them. Packed. I get up this morning, I turn on one of the networks, and they show an empty field. I say, wait a minute, I made a speech. I looked out, the field was – it looked like a million, million and a half people. They showed a field where there were practically nobody standing there. And they said, Donald Trump did not draw well. …

But, you know, we have something that's amazing because we had – it looked – honestly, it looked like a million and a half people. Whatever it was, it was. But it went all the way back to the Washington Monument. And I turn on – and by mistake I get this network, and it showed an empty field. And it said we drew 250,000 people. Now, that's not bad, but it's a lie. We had 250,000 people literally around – you know, in the little bowl that we constructed. That was 250,000 people. The rest of the 20-block area, all the way back to the Washington Monument, was packed. So we caught them, and we caught them in a beauty. And I think they're going to pay a big price.

– **Trump at CIA Headquarters in Langley, Virginia on January 21, 2017 (National Security & Defense).**

T-Brain's Two-Cents: **Trumpy,** I'll take it from here… In summary: **Me speech good, me audience biggest, you pay big. Period**.

".@PressSec Spicer: This was the largest audience to ever witness an inauguration, period."

(@VOANews)
Jan 21, 2017, 3:03 PM. Tweet

"Wow, television ratings just out: 31 million people watched the Inauguration, 11 million more than the very good ratings from 4 years ago!"

(@realDonaldTrump)
Jan 22, 2017, 4:51 AM. Tweet

T-Brain's Two-Cents: Oops. Technically right but kinda misleading.

"Trump also boasted about the number of people who watched his inaugural on television, saying [in a tweet], 'Wow, television ratings just out: 31 million people watched… [The remainder of this tweet is right above]!'

"The Nielsen television rating service said the 30.6 million who watched Trump's ascent to power topped the 20.6 million figure for former President Barack Obama's inauguration to a second term in 2013, but fell 19 percent short of the 37.8 million who watched Obama's first inauguration in 2009. More Americans typically watch inaugurations when a new president takes office, with the biggest number - 41.8 million - recorded in 1981 when Ronald Reagan was inaugurated for the first of his two terms.

"Trump said on a visit Saturday to the Central Intelligence Agency that the news media lied about the size of the crowd that watched him assume power. Numerous media outlets in the U.S. showed vast swaths of the National Mall vacant as he was sworn into office, compared to pictures of shoulder-to-shoulder crowds at the two Obama inaugurations. … Trump, apparently worried about attempts to delegitimize his presidency, said one television network showed 'an empty field' and reported that he drew just 250,000 people to his inauguration."

– Reported by *VOA News* on January 22, 2017 and includes
Trump commenting on his inauguration's crowd size.

"New White House press secretary Sean Spicer, widely criticized for his assessment of the crowd size at President Donald Trump's swearing-in last Friday [January 20, 2017], said Monday 'it's unquestionable' that the event was the 'largest watched inaugural ever.' Spicer said 'tens of millions' of people watched Trump's assumption of power on social media and online streaming by news networks, in addition to the 30.6 million viewers on U.S. television networks and perhaps a few hundred thousand at the event in Washington. Late Saturday [January 21, 2017], Spicer told reporters, 'This was the largest audience to ever witness an inauguration, period, both in person and around the globe.'

"He offered no documentation for the claim and took no questions from reporters. But his statements on the size of the crowd mirrored Trump's earlier boast that perhaps as many as 1.5 million watched from the National Mall in Washington as he was sworn in as the country's 45th president. ...

"The U.S. government no longer makes crowd estimates for large gatherings on the National Mall, after feuding for years with groups staging events that often claimed bigger crowds than the officials said had shown up. But virtually all U.S. media accounts concluded that far fewer people attended Trump's inauguration, compared to those in 2009 and 2013 for former President Barack Obama.

"Widely published photos of Obama's 2009 swearing-in, when he started his first four year term, compared with Trump's inauguration showed a much larger crowd eight years ago, with large swaths of the National Mall nearly empty last Friday [January 20, 2017]. An estimated 1.8 million people jammed the mall for Obama's first inauguration, while one television network estimated Trump's crowd at 250,000, although some estimated a bigger crowd."

"Whatever the Friday number, other analysts said many more people attended Saturday's [January 21, 2017] Women's March on Washington, a celebrity studded event intended as a rebuke to Trump's ascent to power. ... Kellyanne Conway, another Trump aide, said Sunday that Spicer was offering 'alternative facts' about the crowd size, but repeatedly declined to say why Trump ordered his press secretary to make the erroneous crowd statements."

– Reported by *VOA News* on January 22, 2017 and includes comments from White House press secretary Sean Spicer and White House advisor Kellyanne Conway about the crowd size of President Trump's inauguration ceremony.

T-Brain's Two-Cents: K-Con, I love how you alternative-spun Spicey's alternative-facts! Brilliant alternative-smoke-and-mirrors!

T-Brain's Two-Cents: Hey... Wait!! Did Spicey just come clean?!?:

Recent news shed light on how certain individuals viewed this inauguration crowd matter more recently.

– By January 2018 there were numerous news articles on this topic – including some articles by *The Hill* dated January 4, 22 and 29, 2018.

> **T-Brain's Two-Cents: Trumpy,** if these are accurate… then me thinks we may have been off on our inaugural crowd count by **A LOT!**
>
> thehill.com/blogs/blog-briefing-room/news/367490-spicer-i-screwed-up-in-comments-about-inauguration-crowd-size
>
> thehill.com/homenews/administration/370214-trump-regretted-fighting-media-over-inauguration-crowd-size-book
>
> thehill.com/homenews/administration/371250-spicer-i-regret-embarrassing-myself-and-my-family

---

Nervous Tick About The Mueller Investigation?

"FBI Agent Peter Strzok (on the Mueller team) should have recused himself on day one. He was out to STOP THE ELECTION OF DONALD TRUMP. He needed an insurance policy. Those are illegal, improper goals, trying to influence the Election. He should never, ever been allowed to…….."

(@realDonaldTrump)
Aug 1, 2018, 6:03 AM. Tweet

"…..remain in the FBI while he himself was being investigated. This is a real issue. It won't go into a Mueller Report because Mueller is going to protect these guys. Mueller has an interest in creating the illusion of objectivity around his investigation." ALAN DERSHOWITZ…."

(@realDonaldTrump)
Aug 1, 2018, 6:15 AM. Tweet

"..This is a terrible situation and Attorney General Jeff Sessions should stop this Rigged Witch Hunt right now, before it continues to stain our country any further. Bob Mueller is totally conflicted, and his 17 Angry Democrats that are doing his dirty work are a disgrace to USA!"

(@realDonaldTrump)
Aug 1, 2018, 6:24 AM. Tweet

"Paul Manafort worked for Ronald Reagan, Bob Dole and many other highly prominent and respected political leaders. He worked for me for a very short time. Why didn't government tell me that he was under investigation. These old charges have nothing to do with Collusion - a Hoax!"

(@realDonaldTrump)
Aug 1, 2018, 6:34 AM. Tweet

"Russian Collusion with the Trump Campaign, one of the most successful in history, is a TOTAL HOAX. The Democrats paid for the phony and discredited Dossier which was, along with Comey, McCabe, Strzok and his lover, the lovely Lisa Page, used to begin the Witch Hunt. Disgraceful!"

(@realDonaldTrump)
Aug 1, 2018, 7:01 AM. Tweet

"Looking back on history, who was treated worse, Alfonse Capone, legendary mob boss, killer and "Public Enemy Number One," or Paul Manafort, political operative & Reagan/Dole darling, now serving solitary confinement - although convicted of nothing? Where is the Russian Collusion?"

(@realDonaldTrump)
Aug 1, 2018, 8:35 AM. Tweet

T-Brain's Two-Cents: Well, some might disagree but… **Trumpy** and I think that nothing says more about our **manliness** and saying "**I don't care**" than half a dozen tweets first thing in the morning! (*Actually*, you should just **#ManUp** since this is all kinda unflattering.)

T-Brain's Two-Cents: Folks!! For the 10th time, **Trumpy** just wants this corrupt (his opinion?) investigation to just be allowed to finish!!

PRESS: Thanks a lot, Sarah. There was reaction to the President's tweets today from some of his allies on Capitol Hill. Republican Senator Hatch said, "I don't fully get what he's trying to do." And another Republican senator, Senator Thune, said the Mueller investigation needs to move forward. He said they ought to let them complete their work. Do you agree with that sentiment expressed by Senator Thune that this investigation by Mr. Mueller ought to be completed and not be sort of cut off at its (inaudible)?

SANDERS: We certainly think it should be completed. We'd like it to be completed sooner rather than later. It's gone on for an extensive amount of time. They've still come up with nothing in regards to the President. We'd like to see it come to a close. We've said that a number of times. So, sure, we actually agree on that front.

…

PRESS: Sarah, to follow up on Jon Decker's question. You want the investigation to end. You want it to end, I presume, also without any obstruction, meaning without any interference. Many have described the President's tweet this morning as blowing off steam. Is that a fair characterization? It's just an opinion he's throwing out there; it has nothing to do with his actual governmental control of, or supervision of, this investigation?

SANDERS: Once again, as I said earlier, the President is stating his opinion. It's not an order. But he's been, I think, crystal clear about how he feels about this investigation from the beginning.

PRESS: Can I follow up on that? Because you had said a moment ago that the investigation itself is corrupt, the Mueller investigation. And then you mentioned Comey and McCabe and Strzok. They're not — Strzok certainly isn't anymore. He was for a time.

SANDERS: The entire investigation is based off a dirty, discredited dossier that was paid for by an opposing campaign and had a lot of corruption within the entity which was overseeing it, which was Peter Strzok, James Comey, Andrew McCabe. We've laid this out a number of times. I don't think that we have to go into it every single time we're in here.

PRESS: If it is corrupt, why doesn't the President just end it, or use the powers he has to end it?

SANDERS: Once again, the President has allowed this —

PRESS: If he believes that, why doesn't he follow through on that?

SANDERS: Once again, the President has allowed this process to play out, but he think it's time for it to come to an end.

Sara, go ahead.

PRESS: Thank you, Sarah. I'm just wondering if you can clarify what — this tweet from this morning. Is it the President's desire for, first, Sessions to un-recuse himself from the probe? And is it also his desire for the Special Counsel to be fired?

SANDERS: I think I've clarified this about 10 times now. It's the President's opinion. I don't have anything further.

– Press Secretary Sarah Sanders at a press briefing beginning at 1:32 PM EDT on August 1, 2018 in James S. Brady Press Briefing Room (Whitehouse.gov).

E. Underlying Feelings of Weakness?

Underlying Feelings Of Insecurity?

T-Brain's Two-Cents: **Trumpy**, you sound weak here. **#ManUp!**

"So a reporter for Time magazine – and I have been on there cover, like, 14 or 15 times. I think we have the all-time record in the history of Time Magazine. Like, if Tom Brady is on the cover, it's one time, because he won the Super Bowl or something, right? (Laughter.) I've been on it for 15 times this year. I don't think that's a record, Mike, that can ever be broken. Do you agree with that? What do you think?"

– Trump at CIA Headquarters in Langley, Virginia beginning at 3:21 PM EST on January 21, 2017 (National Security & Defense).

The "Everyone-Worked-Hard-And-I-Was-A-Team-Player-And-So-It's-The-Best-Thing-To-Happen-As-I-Said-Before" Speech

PRESIDENT: So what would be really good, with no Democrat support, is if the Democrats, when it explodes – which it will soon – if they got together with us and got a real healthcare bill. I would be totally up to do it. And I think that's going to happen. I think the losers are Nancy Pelosi and Chuck Schumer, because now they own Obamacare. They own it -- 100 percent own it.

And this is not a Republican healthcare, this is not anything but a Democrat healthcare. And they have Obamacare for a little while longer, until it ceases to exist, which it will at some point in the near future. And just remember this is not our bill, this is their bill.

Now, when they all become civilized and get together, and try and work out a great healthcare bill for the people of this country, we're open to it. We're totally open to it.

I want to thank the Republican Party. I want to thank Paul Ryan – he worked very, very hard, I will tell you that. He worked very, very hard. Tom Price and Mike Pence – who's right here – our Vice President, our great Vice President. Everybody worked hard. I worked as a team player and would have loved to have seen it passed. But again, I think you know I was very clear, I think there wasn't a speech I made, or very few where I didn't mention that perhaps the best thing that can happen is exactly what happened today, because we'll end up with a truly great healthcare bill in the future, after this mess known as Obamacare explodes.

So I want to thank everybody for being here. It will go very smoothly, I really believe. I think this is something -- it certainly was an interesting period of time. We all learned a lot. We learned a lot about loyalty. We learned a lot about the vote-getting process. We learned a lot about some very arcane rules in, obviously, both the Senate and in the House. So it's been -- certainly for me, it's been a very interesting experience. But in the end, I think it's going to be an experience that leads to an even better healthcare plan.

– **Trump in the Oval Office beginning at 4:26 PM EDT on March 24, 2017 (Whitehouse.gov).**

T-Brain's Two-Cents: I told him to shut it but he said he got it. Well, here's **Trumpy**-a-la-naturale speaking to the press after House Republicans withdrew their legislation to repeal and replace Obamacare from a scheduled floor vote that day! (**Oopsie!**) And the quote above is **archived** online (link below) since this transcript was removed afterward from Whitehouse.gov. Kinda embarrassing, no?

web.archive.org/web/20170324223608/https://www.whitehouse.gov/the-press-office/2017/03/24/remarks-president-trump-health-care-bill

CHAPTER FIVE

EXTREME EXRA PERSONALITIES?

"A few isolated groups in the backwater of American life still hold perverted notions of what America is all about. Recently in some places in the nation there's been a disturbing reoccurrence of bigotry and violence. If I may, from the platform of this organization, known for its tolerance, I would like to address a few remarks to those groups who still adhere to senseless racism and religious prejudice, to those individuals who persist in such hateful behavior.

"If I were speaking to them instead of to you, I would say to them, 'You are the ones who are out of step with our society. You are the ones who willfully violate the meaning of the dream that is America. And this country, because of what it stands for, will not stand for your conduct.' My administration will vigorously investigate and prosecute those who, by violence or intimidation, would attempt to deny Americans their constitutional rights."

– President Ronald Reagan in his address at the Annual Convention of the National Association for the Advancement of Colored People (NAACP) in Denver, Colorado on June 29, 1981 (Ronald Reagan Presidential Library).

T-Brain's Two-Cents: Thank you for those remarkable words, President Regan. Rest in peace. And here is his entire speech:

www.reaganlibrary.gov/research/speeches/62981a

A. Extra Fragile Self-Image?

I'm Smart Enough, Gosh Darn It, Even Losers Should Like Me

In a pre-presidency tweet, Trump remarked that his I.Q. was one of the highest and that others – or as he calls them, "losers and haters" – should not blame themselves for, as he further articulated, their own insecurities and stupidity since it is presumably not their fault.

– Trump tweeted on May 8, 2018 at 6:37 PM.

T-Brain's Two-Cents: Well, one can still easily find this "beauty" of a **Trumpy** tweet by simply **googling** in a single search these key words altogether and as shown without any quotation marks:

sorry trump you stupid and insecure tweet 2013

T-Brain's Two-Cents: Hmm. Kinda awkward as **Trumpy's** brain that I have to admit this but… This is all I got out of these these next two blabbering tweets from our adorable **President Numnuts**: '**ACTUALLY**… blah, blah.. **VERY**… blah, blah… **NOT SMART'**

"….Actually, throughout my life, my two greatest assets have been mental stability and being, like, really smart. Crooked Hillary Clinton also played these cards very hard and, as everyone knows, went down in flames. I went from VERY successful businessman, to top T.V. Star….."

(@realDonaldTrump)
Jan 6, 2018, 4:27 AM. Tweet

"....to President of the United States (on my first try). I think that would qualify as not smart, but genius....and a very stable genius at that!"

(@realDonaldTrump)
Jan 6, 2018, 4:30 AM. Tweet

Went To *2 Colleges* But Only 1 Was An Ivy & Yet He's Still Smart?

PRESS: Mr. President, you were talking about the policy issues that you all were focusing on the last few days here at Camp David, but this morning you were tweeting about your mental state. Why did you feel the need to tweet about that this morning?

PRESIDENT: Well, only because I went to the best colleges for college [Note: In the audio version he appears to instead say, "the best colleges, or college"]. I went to a — I had a situation where I was a very excellent student. Came out and made billions and billions of dollars. Became one of the top businesspeople. Went to television and, for ten years, was a tremendous success, as you probably have heard. Ran for President one time and won.

And then I hear this guy [Michael Wolff, author of "Fire and Fury: Inside the Trump White House"] that does not know me, doesn't know me at all. By the way, did not interview me for three — he said he interviewed me for three hours in the White House. It didn't exist, okay? It's in his imagination.

– Trump at Camp David in Hauvers, Maryland beginning at 12:00 PM EST on January 6, 2018 (Whitehouse.gov).

T-Brain's Two-Cents: Here's **Trumpy** after the Congressional Republican Leadership Retreat. My one-word reaction … **Ooof.** And in case readers didn't know: **Trumpy** went to Fordham University for two years and then transferred to the University of Pennsylvania to finish his last 2 years of **college**. And that was... it for Mr. SmartyPants.

No Self-Image Issues Since Obviously They Have Good Taste?

PRESS: (Inaudible) and did you meet Chris Christie here, yesterday?

PRESIDENT: Well, we're looking at other people. I did not see Chris Christie yesterday. I heard he was in the White House. He's a friend of mine. He's a good man. When he got out of the presidential race, as you know, the next day he supported me. He has good taste. So he proved one thing: He has good taste. But when he got out, he immediately supported me. I like Chris Christie, but I have not talked to him about it. He was in the White House yesterday, but I did not see him.

– **Trump on the South Lawn beginning at 9:05 AM EST on November 9, 2018 (Whitehouse.gov).**

T-Brain's Two-Cents: **Trumpy** may have intentionally rambled here to hide that he may have been really really hungry and wanted to have a little **taste** of something. I think. Regardless, he's clearly a **Master Rambler**... and he doesn't even have to try that hard! **Talentísimo!**

Wait, There Is No Longer A 'Man-Child Of The Year' Issue?

PRESS: A question about the recently released Time Magazine online poll. Who do you feel – obviously, I can assume who you think deserves to be first place. Who do you think deserves to be second place as Time's Person of the Year?

PRESIDENT: It's called "Person of the Year," right?

PRESS: Yeah.

PRESIDENT: It's no longer "Man of the Year," right?

PRESS: Yeah. Their language.

PRESIDENT: I don't know. That's up to Time Magazine. I've been there before. I can't imagine anybody else other than Trump. Can you imagine anybody other than Trump? Huh?

– **Trump on the South Lawn beginning at 3:11 P.M. EST on November 20, 2018 (Whitehouse.gov).**

T-Brain's Two-Cents: Actually, I can imagine someone or something else on the front cover other than you: **ME**, your liddle' organ that is technically a brain. And I made you, **Trumpmunch**.

No Self-Image Issues Since Obviously They Have Good Taste?

"While the Fake News loves to talk about my so-called low approval rating, @foxandfriends just showed that my rating on Dec. 28, 2017, was approximately the same as President Obama on Dec. 28, 2009, which was 47%...and this despite massive negative Trump coverage & Russia hoax!"

(@realDonaldTrump)
Dec 29, 2017, 4:46 AM. Tweet

T-Brain's Two-Cents: Trumpster, let me put it in simple terms for you: Just like your **face's skin tone** appears to be an outlier at times… this poll you're quoting also appears to be an outlier at times. Does that help? Or don't take my word for it… you can just read below:

"Trump's holiday Twitter feed also touted a new poll suggesting his approval rating was improving. The Rasmussen Poll, which is seen as an outlier that regularly shows the president's numbers higher than others, showed him at 46 percent approval among Americans. That would be a significant jump from other polls that show an approval rating in the mid-30s, which is the lowest of any president since polling began."

– **Reported by *VOA News* on December 29, 2017 and in regards to a Trump tweet from December 29, 2017 at 4:46 AM (as shown on the previous page). This *VOA News* article further explains this polling data by the Rasmussen Poll.**

B. Extra Magical Thinking?

A 'Magical' Snapshot Leading Up To 2018 Midterm Election?

"Republicans are doing so well in early voting, and at the polls, and now this "Bomb" stuff happens and the momentum greatly slows - news not talking politics. Very unfortunate, what is going on. Republicans, go out and vote!"

(@realDonaldTrump)
Oct 26, 2018, 7:19 AM. Tweet

T-Brain's Two-Cents: Hey, **Surly Don**, talking about this 'stuff' this way isn't cool. It's kinda obvious what you're doing when you're referring to those packages with explosive devices that were sent from some **loser** (Trump supporter?) and mailed to national figures and Democrats who were critical of you. **Trumpet**, you should just **chill**.

'Magical' Snapshots Of Aftermath Of 2018 Midterm Election?

PRESIDENT: Thank you. Thank you very much. Please, thank you.

It was a big day yesterday. An incredible day. And last night, the Republican Party defied history to expand our Senate Majority while significantly beating expectations in the House for the midtown and midterm year. We did this in spite of a very dramatic fundraising disadvantage driven by Democrats' wealthy donors and special interests, and very hostile media coverage, to put it mildly. The media coverage set a new record and a new standard.

We also had a staggering number of House retirements. So it's a little tough. These are seats that could've been held pretty easily, and we had newcomers going in, and a lot of them worked very hard. But it's very difficult when you have that many retirements.

We held a large number of campaign rallies with large, large numbers of people going to every one — and to the best of my knowledge, we didn't have a vacant or an empty seat; I'm sure you would have reported it if you spotted one — including 30 rallies in the last 60 days. And we saw the candidates that I supported achieve great success last night.

As an example, of the 11 candidates we campaigned with during the last week, 9 won last night. This vigorous campaigning stopped the blue wave that they talked about. I don't know if there ever was such a thing, but could've been. If we didn't do the campaign, probably there could've been. And the history really will see what a good job we did in the final couple of weeks in terms of getting some tremendous people over the finish line. They really are tremendous people, but many of them were not known. But they will be known.

This election marks the largest Senate gains for a President's party in a first midterm election since at least President Kennedy's in 1962.

There have been only four midterm elections since 1934 in which a President's party has gained even a single Senate seat. As of now, we picked up, it looks like, three. Could be four. Perhaps it could be two. But we picked up a lot. And most likely, that number will be three. You people probably know that better than I do at this point, because you've looked at the more recent numbers.

– Trump in the East Room of the White House beginning at 11:57 AM EST on November 7, 2018 (Whitehouse.gov.)

T-Brain's Two-Cents: Phew!! What a relief! I thought you would've been pissed with the 2018 midterm results. Glad *you* think it went well!

T-Brain's Two-Cents: Well, not everyone (even in your own party!) agrees with you. **Oopsie** on comprehension, you **Liddle' Dummy**. I guess even going to 2 colleges didn't help. Maybe it confused you more.

[*VOA News*:] "Women in key swing districts across the country delivered congressional victories to the Democratic Party Tuesday [November 6, 2018], helping to shift the balance of power in the U.S. House of Representatives for the remaining two years of the Trump presidency.

"The U.S. may be divided along political and ideological lines, but Associated Press exit polls show female voters united behind the Democratic Party in the 2018 midterm congressional elections by a 55 percent to 41 percent margin. The partisan divide among male voters was much narrower.

"In a midterm election cycle heralded as the 'Year of the Woman' because of the record number of female candidates for office and the surging #MeToo movement, women delivered a generally harsh verdict regarding Trump's first two years in office. ...

"Republican Sen. Lindsey Graham told Fox News Tuesday [November 6, 2018] night after projections showed Republicans had lost control of the House. '[The problem involving suburban women needs to be addressed since it is real],' he said."

– Reported by *VOA News* on Nov. 6, 2018 regarding a *Fox News* interview with Sen. Lindsey Graham (R-SC).

PRESIDENT: And again, I'm very honored to be with all of you. It was a great day yesterday. It was a great evening. I think we had a tremendous success. And hopefully the tone can get better. Hopefully —

PRESS: How will you change that?

PRESIDENT: Hopefully the tone can get a lot better. And I really believe it begins with the media. I really — we used to call it the "press." But I really —

PRESS: Does it begin with you, Mr. President?

PRESIDENT: But I really believe it begins with the media. If you would cover — and there was a very interesting story written in a very good paper recently that talked about the fact that it isn't good what the media is doing, and that I do have the right to fight back because I'm treated very unfairly.

So I do fight back. And I'm fighting back not for me; I'm fighting back for the people of this country.

Thank you all very much. Thank you.

– Trump in the East Room of the White House beginning at 11:57 AM EST on November 7, 2018 (Whitehouse.gov).

T-Brain's Two-Cents: There you go again, **Liddle' Donny**, making up for whatever you want as if you were a seven-year old liddle' rich brat. **CORRECTION**… liddle' brat whose father was the rich one.

"Law Enforcement is looking into another big corruption scandal having to do with Election Fraud in #Broward and Palm Beach. Florida voted for Rick Scott!"

**(@realDonaldTrump)
Nov 8, 2018, 6:38 AM. Tweet**

T-Brain's Two-Cents: **Trumpy** tells me that none of this vote counting concerns him. Nonevent, people! **Trumpy** just wants to share his thoughtful opinion to all during his allotted Executive Time.

"You mean they are just now finding votes in Florida and Georgia – but the Election was on Tuesday? Let's blame the Russians and demand an immediate apology from President Putin!"

(@realDonaldTrump)
Nov 9, 2018, 7:58 AM. Tweet

"As soon as Democrats sent their best Election stealing lawyer, Marc Elias, to Broward County they miraculously started finding Democrat votes. Don't worry, Florida - I am sending much better lawyers to expose the FRAUD!"

(@realDonaldTrump)
Nov 9, 2018, 8:52 AM. Tweet

"Rick Scott was up by 50,000+ votes on Election Day, now they "found" many votes and he is only up 15,000 votes. "The Broward Effect." How come they never find Republican votes?"

(@realDonaldTrump)
Nov 9, 2018, 9:36 AM. Tweet

"In the 2016 Election I was winning by so much in Florida that Broward County, which was very late with vote tabulation and probably getting ready to do a "number," couldn't do it because not enough people live in Broward for them to falsify a victory!"

(@realDonaldTrump)
Nov 9, 2018, 10:20 AM. Tweet

"Scott has asked the Florida Department of Law Enforcement to investigate the election departments in South Florida's Democratic-leaning Broward and Palm Beach counties after his lead narrowed as ballots continued to be counted throughout the week. A state election spokeswoman said Friday [November 9, 2018], however, an investigation would not be launched because there was no evidence of fraud."

– Reported by *VOA News* on November 10, 2018 and in regards to Republican Governor Rick Scott asking the Florida Department of Law Enforcement (FDLE) to investigate any fraudulent activity during the November 6, 2018 midterm election.

T-Brain's Two-Cents: Again…**Trumpy** just totally totally doesn't care about any of this. He embodies **steel courage** and anyone who disagrees is pathetic and a loser but it's not their fault.

"Trying to STEAL two big elections in Florida! We are watching closely!"

**(@realDonaldTrump)
Nov 10, 2018, 11:09 AM. Tweet**

"The Florida Election should be called in favor of Rick Scott and Ron DeSantis in that large numbers of new ballots showed up out of nowhere, and many ballots are missing or forged. An honest vote count is no longer possible-ballots massively infected. Must go with Election Night!"

(@realDonaldTrump)
Nov 12, 2018, 4:44 AM. Tweet

A 10-day extension is afforded to military and overseas voters from Florida under certain guidelines, including a requirement that the overseas voter's vote-by-mail ballot be postmarked by the election date and received within 10 days.

– Paraphrased from the Website of the Florida Division of Elections.

T-Brain's Two-Cents: Uh oh!! **Donny Boy**, I think it's a **Code Red** (maybe more **Orange-ish**, no?) **Situation**. I guess late incoming votes can be legit! Here's a link to the **Florida Division of Elections**:

dos.myflorida.com/elections/for-voters/voting/military-and-overseas-citizens-voting/

Yikes! That means for the 11/**6**/18 midterm election such ballots could still be accepted until 11/**16**/18 if postmarked by 11/6/18! Oops

"When will Bill Nelson concede in Florida? The characters running Broward and Palm Beach voting will not be able to "find" enough votes, too much spotlight on them now!"

(@realDonaldTrump)
Nov 13, 2018, 8:32 AM. Tweet

C. Extremely Self-Absorbed?

Quite Simply… 'Self-Absorbed'?

"Beautiful weather all over our great country, a perfect day for all Women to March. Get out there now to celebrate the historic milestones and unprecedented economic success and wealth creation that has taken place over the last 12 months. Lowest female unemployment in 18 years!"

(@realDonaldTrump)
Jan 20, 2018, 10:51 AM. Tweet

T-Brain's Two-Cents: Let me take it from here, **Donny**… Ladies, thank you for obviously marching for all that Donny kinda sorta did for you. (**NOT**) And at least I (**T-Brain**) think that it's so amazing that there were somehow more people that marched that day than there were that showed up for **Trumpy's** inauguration. (**Kinda Awkward**.)

Quite Versatile: Going From 'Self-Absorbed' To 'Self-Dealing'?

PRESS: The Washington Post, in a statement – put out a statement – they said that you're putting your personal interests, your commercial interests ahead of national interests.

TRUMP: Well, I have nothing to do with Saudi — just so you understand, I don't make deals with Saudi Arabia. I don't have money from Saudi Arabia. I have nothing to do with Saudi Arabia. I couldn't care less.

And I will tell you, and as most of you know, being President has cost me a fortune, and that's okay with me. I knew that a long time ago. But being President has cost me a fortune — a tremendous fortune like you've never seen before, but someday I'll tell you what that is.

But – and I knew that a long time ago because I don't do deals. I don't do – all I do is focus on this country and making great deals for this country. I don't focus on making on great deals for myself because I don't care anymore.

So, Saudi Arabia has nothing to do with me. What does have to do with me is putting America first.

– Trump at the South Lawn beginning at 3:11 P.M. EST on November 20, 2018 (Whitehouse.gov).

T-Brain's Two-Cents: Yes, people need to understand that this presidency may cost **Trumpy's** daddy a ton of his fortune which someday **Trumpy** may or may not tell you. **#QuestionablySelfMade**

D. Extremely Insensitive To Others?

Oh-such-yugely-dumb-ass-sphincter-boy-says-the-word-What?

T-Brain's Two-Cents: **Trumpy,** whatever you do… DON'T START WITH THE WORD… "**WHAT**"! (Argh… Too late! Here you go with all of these asinine tweets!)

"What is the purpose of the House doing good immigration bills when you need 9 votes by Democrats in the Senate, and the Dems are only looking to Obstruct (which they feel is good for them in the Mid-Terms). Republicans must get rid of the stupid Filibuster Rule-it is killing you!"

(@realDonaldTrump)
June 21, 2018, 6:08 AM. Tweet

"What's going on at @CNN is happening, to different degrees, at other networks - with @NBCNews being the worst. The good news is that Andy Lack(y) is about to be fired(?) for incompetence, and much worse. When Lester Holt got caught fudging my tape on Russia, they were hurt badly!"

(@realDonaldTrump)
Aug 30, 2018, 4:02 AM. Tweet

"What was Nike thinking?"

(@realDonaldTrump)
Sept 7, 2018, 3:56 AM. Tweet

The No-I'm-Not-Dumb-You're-Dumb Presidential Treatment?

"I heard poorly rated @Morning_Joe speaks badly of me (don't watch anymore). Then how come low I.Q. Crazy Mika, along with Psycho Joe, came.."

(@realDonaldTrump)
June 29, 2017, 5:52 AM. Tweet

"...to Mar-a-Lago 3 nights in a row around New Year's Eve, and insisted on joining me. She was bleeding badly from a face-lift. I said no!"

(@realDonaldTrump)
June 29, 2017, 5:58 AM. Tweet

T-Brain's Two-Cents: Ahhh… **Trumpmunch,** you need to let go at times or people will start calling you **Deranged Donald.** (Too late!)

"Mr. President, your tweet was beneath the office and represents what is wrong with American politics, not the greatness of America."

(@LindseyGrahamSC)
June 29, 2017, 7:15 AM. Tweet

"This has to stop – we all have a job – 3 branches of gov't and media. We don't have to get along, but we must show respect and civility."

(@SenatorCollins)
June 29, 2017, 8:18 AM. Tweet

Astoundingly (Orange-)'Tone-Deaf'?

"And I just want to thank you because you're very, very special people. You were here long before any of us were here, although we have a representative in Congress who, they say, was here a long time ago. They call her 'Pocahontas.' But you know what, I like you because you are special. You are special people. You are really incredible people."

– Trump in the Oval Office beginning at 2:27 PM EST on November 27, 2017 (Whitehouse.gov).

T-Brain's Two-Cents: Well, I'm not sure if you saying this to those three +90-year old Navajo code talkers to honor Navajo veterans was as well received… when you kinda referenced Sen. Warren that way. Just next time, **Donny**, maybe keep it professional and not personal?

'Not-Said-In-Public-But-No-One-But-Him-Denies-It' Quote?

T-Brain's Two-Cents: Alright here we go…. "**Sh*thole countries**" was reportedly said by **Trumpy** and it's the only quote in this novel that was not made in a public setting by **The Trumpet**. But T-Brain (yes, I speak in the third-person, too) decided to still include it as the sole exception to the novel's only-public-comments-by-**Trumpmunch** rule since this comment was admonished by oh-so many Republicans and the White House didn't even deny such a derogatory comment was made at that meeting!!

"President Donald Trump stunned lawmakers in a White House meeting on immigration Thursday [January 11, 2018] when he reportedly referred to Haiti and African nations as 's---hole countries.' 'Why are we having all these people from s---hole countries come here,' the president asked as was first reported by media including The Washington Post, The New York Times and CNN. The crude term means dirty and impoverished. Trump said the United States should let in more people from places such as Norway, whose prime minister met with him in the White House Wednesday.

"After being asked by media, including VOA, to respond, White House spokesperson Raj Shah issued a statement saying the president will only accept an immigration deal that 'adequately addresses the visa lottery system and chain migration ...' Chain migration is a term used by immigration critics to refer to the system that allows relatives to sponsor family members to come to the United States. Shah's statement did not deny reports that the president used crude language when talking about Haiti and Africa.

"VOA also reached out to the offices of U.S. lawmakers who were reportedly present at the meeting. Aides to lawmakers who attended the meeting declined to provide comment on Trump's remarks, according to the Associated Press.

"Trump reportedly made the remark as Sen. Dick Durbin, a Democrat from Illinois, was explaining the outlines of an agreement reached by six bipartisan senators that would protect nearly 800,000 young immigrants from deportation as well as bolster border security, according to the Post. ...

"By late Thursday [January 10, 2019], lawmakers were reacting to the reported comments. ... Republican Rep. Mia Love, whose family came from Haiti, said the president's comments are 'unkind, divisive, elitist, and fly in the face of our nation's values. This behavior is unacceptable from the leader of our nation.' Love, of Utah, called on Trump to apologize to the people of Haiti.

"Utah Sen. Orrin Hatch, also a Republican, said he wanted more details 'regarding the president's comments.' 'Part of what makes America so special is that we welcome the best and brightest in the world, regardless of their country of origin,' Hatch added.

"Arizona Sen. Jeff Flake, a Republican, tweeted late Thursday, 'My ancestors came from countries not nearly as prosperous as the one we live in today. I'm glad that they were welcomed here.'

– Reported by *VOA News* on January 11, 2018 regarding Trump in a meeting with lawmakers to discuss immigration.

T-Brain's Two-Cents: Oof. Even **Lookie-Me-Lindsey** had a few words to say about this, **Trumpy**. He's one of your favorites, too.

"The comments, first reported Thursday [January 11, 2018] by The Washington Post, were made during a presentation by Durbin and Republican Senator Lindsey Graham about bipartisan legislation to protect from deportation those immigrants who were illegally brought to the U.S. as children by their parents. Durbin noted that Graham confronted the president about his remarks."

– Reported by *VOA News* on Jan. 12, 2018 and regarding how Sen. Lindsey Graham (R-SC) presumably confronted Trump about certain comments.

T-Brain's Two-Cents: Oh! Now you kinda sorta kinda come clean to the public, **Donny-Tough-Guy**? Was it because of **Lindsey-Boo**?

"The language used by me at the DACA meeting was tough, but this was not the language used. What was really tough was the outlandish proposal made - a big setback for DACA!"

(@realDonaldTrump)
Jan 12, 2018, 4:28 AM. Tweet

"Never said anything derogatory about Haitians other than Haiti is, obviously, a very poor and troubled country. Never said "take them out." Made up by Dems. I have a wonderful relationship with Haitians. Probably should record future meetings - unfortunately, no trust!"

(@realDonaldTrump)
Jan 12, 2018, 5:48 AM. Tweet

"President Donald Trump is continuing to push back against lawmakers and others who have taken issue with a vulgar comment he is said to have made last week during a meeting with senators on immigration reform. ... During last Thursday's Oval Office meeting, Trump was reported to have referred to immigrants from Haiti, El Salvador and Africa as coming from 's---hole countries.'

"The reporter for The Washington Post, Josh Dawsey, who first wrote about Trump's use of the vulgarity, told CNN on Monday that White House officials now say Trump might have uttered a slightly different profanity, questioning why the United States was accepting immigrants from 's---house countries.' ...

"The president on Sunday [January 14, 2018] denied he is a racist, telling reporters at his Mar-a-Lago resort in the state of Florida: 'I am the least racist person you will ever interview.' According to some in the room during a White House meeting last week on immigration, Trump asked why the U.S. is letting in immigrants from Haiti, El Salvador and Africa and said he wanted more from countries such as Norway. He also apparently said he wants to exclude Haiti from an immigration reform deal."

– Reported by *VOA News* on January 14, 2018 regarding Trump comments from Mar-a-Lago in Palm Beach, FL about the January 11, 2018 meeting with lawmakers to discuss immigration.

Official Discriminationy Types of Acts By Presidential Decree?

"[Sessions] said he 'understands the history of civil rights and the horrendous impact that relentless and systematic discrimination and the denial of voting rights has had on our African-American brothers and sisters.' The country, Sessions said, can never go back, and he vowed to protect equality for every citizen, including gays and transgenders — although he has voted against various bills aimed at protecting gay rights during his 20 years in the Senate."

– Reported by *VOA News* on January 10, 2017 about Sen. Jeff Sessions (R-AL) in Washington, D.C. during his second day of Senate Judiciary Committee confirmation hearings on Capitol Hill for his nomination to become U.S. attorney general.

"After consultation with my Generals and military experts, please be advised that the United States Government will not accept or allow......"

(@realDonaldTrump)
July 26, 2017, 5:55 AM. Tweet

"....Transgender individuals to serve in any capacity in the U.S. Military. Our military must be focused on decisive and overwhelming....."

(@realDonaldTrump)
July 26, 2017, 6:04 AM. Tweet

"....victory and cannot be burdened with the tremendous medical costs and disruption that transgender in the military would entail. Thank you"

(@realDonaldTrump)
July 26, 2017, 6:08 AM. Tweet

T-Brain's Two-Cents: Hey, **Donny Douche**, even "your" military appears to disagree with you. Maybe come clean at this point and just admit that you're a... **bigly douche**. As your brain I should know, too.

"The U.S. military's top general says there has been no change yet to the military's policy on transgender personnel, despite President Donald Trump's announcement on Twitter that they will be banned from serving 'in any capacity.' 'There will be no modifications to the current policy until the President's direction has been received by the Secretary of Defense [Jim Mattis] and the Secretary has issued implementation guidance,' the chairman of the Joint Chiefs of Staff, General Joseph Dunford, wrote in a memo obtained by VOA. ... 'In the meantime, we will continue to treat all of our personnel with respect,' Dunford added."

– Reported by *VOA News* on July 27, 2017 about a memo written by General Joseph Dunford, chairman of the Joint Chiefs of Staff.

A number of Pentagon officials and/or Republicans expressed views that appeared to run counter to the views shared by President Trump regarding transgender military individuals.

- These point of views were mentioned in a number of articles, including some by *The Hill* that were dated July 26 and 30, 2017 and August 11, 2017 and September 26, 2017.

T-Brain's Two-Cents: And so many disagree with your 'thinking'!:

thehill.com/homenews/senate/343881-hatch-stands-with-transgender-utahns

thehill.com/policy/defense/344391-trump-transgender-decision-rattles-pentagon

thehill.com/policy/defense/346165-navy-secretary-on-transgender-troops-any-patriot-should-be-allowed-to-serve

thehill.com/policy/defense/352451-top-general-i-advised-that-transgender-troops-shouldnt-be-separated-from

'Many Agree With Me & So It's Okay We Don't Let Those In'?

"What is our country coming to when a judge can halt a Homeland Security travel ban and anyone, even with bad intentions, can come into U.S.?"

(@realDonaldTrump)
Feb 4, 2017, 12:44 PM. Tweet

PRESIDENT: Look, as far as I'm concerned, as to whether or not it's an issue – for those of you that didn't hear – immigration is always tricky, but to me it's not tricky. You have to do the right thing whether there's an election or not.

I'm very tough at the borders. We've been very tough at the borders. People have to come into our country legally, not illegally. Legally. And I want them to come in on merit.

If that's a bad policy, then guess what, a lot of bad things are going to happen. But a lot of people agree with me. I would say a vast majority of our country agrees. They don't want criminals coming into our country. They don't want people that they don't want in the country that aren't going to help us as a country. They don't want these people coming in. So we have a very strong policy.

– Trump at the South Lawn beginning at 3:52 P.M. EDT on October 13, 2018 (Whitehouse.gov).

T-Brain's Two-Cents: When it comes to immigration… Nothing is tricky for Donald. And that includes where his own father was born.

PRESS: Do you regret the ad? Do you regret the ad that you did that was branded as racist ad and even Fox News wouldn't air it?

PRESIDENT: No, I don't. No. No. No.

PRESS: NBC wouldn't air it, and other networks.

PRESIDENT: Do I regret it?

PRESS: Yeah.

PRESIDENT: Surprised you would ask me that question. I do not.

– Trump in the East Room of the White House beginning at 11:57 AM EST on November 7, 2018 (Whitehouse.gov).

T-Brain's Two-Cents: Well, I gotta say… The one most admirable thing about you, Trumpster, is that… there's no fear at telling it at how it is. Hats off to you on that. If you just weren't such a **freakin' liddle' douchebag** you might even be remembered fondly. Not gonna happen. And daddy wouldn't like how you destroyed **his** fortune, too!

PRESS: Sir, last night — in response to last night's "60 Minutes" piece, you said your policy at the border was the same as the Obama administration's. It wasn't. You decided to prosecute —

PRESIDENT: Say it again. What?

PRESS: In response to last night's "60 Minutes" report —

PRESIDENT: Yeah, so I'll tell you what. Obama had a separation policy; we all had the same policy.

PRESS: You did not have — sir, no, you didn't.

PRESIDENT: I tried to do it differently, but Obama had a separation policy. But people don't like to talk about that.

PRESS: Sir, it was different. You decided to prosecute everyone at the border.

– Trump at the South Lawn beginning at 2:44 P.M. EST on November 26, 2018 (Whitehouse.gov).

Everyone Is A Loser Except Presidents That Expect Respect?

PRESS: Mr. President, how long are you going to leave Jim Acosta in the penalty box?

PRESIDENT: I think Jim Acosta is a very unprofessional man. He does this with everybody. He gets paid to do that. You know, he gets paid to burst in. He's a very unprofessional guy. Whether it was me or Ronald Reagan or anybody else, he would have done the same thing.

Look, I don't think he's a smart person, but he's got a loud voice. And —

PRESS: Is it permanent?

PRESIDENT: Wait, wait. David, do you mind if I answer the question?

PRESS: Sure. Of course.

PRESIDENT: And as far as I'm concerned, I haven't made that decision. But it could be others also. When you're in the White House — this is a very sacred place to me. This is a very special place. You have to treat the White House with respect. You have to treat the presidency with respect. If you've ever seen him dealing with Sarah Huckabee Sanders, it's a disgrace. And he does it for, you know, the reason.

The same thing with April Ryan. I watched her get up. I mean, you talk about somebody that's a loser. She doesn't know what the hell she's doing. She gets publicity, and then she gets a pay raise or she gets a contract with, I think, CNN. But she's very nasty, and she shouldn't be. She shouldn't be. You've got to treat the White House and the Office of the Presidency with respect.

– Trump at the South Lawn beginning at 9:05 AM EST on November 9, 2018 (Whitehouse.gov).

T-Brain's Two-Cents: Unprofessional is as unprofessional does.

E. Not The Work At All Of A Great Mind?

Creative Mind Of An Adult-Child's Space Odyssey?

PRESIDENT: My administration is reclaiming America's heritage as the world's greatest space-faring nation. The essence of the American character is to explore new horizons and to tame new frontiers. But our destiny, beyond the Earth, is not only a matter of national identity, but a matter of national security. So important for our military. So important. And people don't talk about it.

When it comes to defending America, it is not enough to merely have an American presence in space. We must have American dominance in space. So important.

Very importantly, I'm here by directing the Department of Defense and Pentagon to immediately begin the process necessary to establish a space force as the sixth branch of the armed forces. That's a big statement.

We are going to have the Air Force and we are going to have the Space Force — separate but equal. It is going to be something. So important. General Dunford, if you would carry that assignment out, I would be very greatly honored, also. Where's General Dunford? General? Got it?

GENERAL DUNFORD: We got it.

PRESIDENT: Let's go get it, General. (Applause.) But that's the importance that we give it. We're going to have the Space Force.

One year ago, I revived the National Space Council and put exactly the right man in charge, and that's our friend, Mike Pence. He feels very strongly about this. And in December, I signed a historic directive that will return Americans to the moon for the first time since 1972, if you can believe that. (Applause.)

...

PRESIDENT: Good luck, General Dunford and the Joint Chiefs. I want to wish you a lot of luck with Space Force. But that shows how important it is. Congratulations on your tremendous success, but you're going to have far more success right now.

Thank you very much. Thank you. Thank you. Thank you, Mike. (Applause.)

– Trump speaking with the National Space Council in the East Room of the White House beginning at 12:15 EDT on June 18, 2018 (Whitehouse.gov).

T-Brain's Two-Cents: But not everyone really toes the line, Trumpy:

"President Donald Trump has repeatedly called for a Space Force as a new military branch that would be 'separate but equal' to the Army, Navy, Air Force, Marine Corps and Coast Guard.

"During a political rally Tuesday [July 31, 2018] in Tampa, Florida, Trump again mentioned that he had directed the Pentagon to begin creating 'the sixth branch of our military — the Space Force.'

"Pentagon spokesman Army Lt. Col. Jamie Davis said Tuesday the Pentagon was in the 'final coordination stages' of the report. A U.S. official told VOA the report should be ready 'in days.'

> "The report was ordered by Congress after Defense Secretary Jim Mattis sent a letter to congressional leaders opposing the creation of a new military branch. In his letter last October, Mattis said he did not see the need for new 'organizational layers at a time when we are focused on reducing overhead and integrating joint warfighting functions.'

A draft report seen by Defense One, a military news-related website, said the Pentagon was prepared to create an 11th unified combatant command by the end of the year to focus on space. U.S. Space Command would be set up similarly to U.S. Special Operations Command, which oversees special forces from various military branches, and U.S. Cyber Command, which oversees cyberspace operations across the military branches.

> Lawmakers in the House Strategic Forces subcommittee have expressed interest not in the creation of a new branch, but in the creation of a new Space Corps within the Air Force.

– Reported by *VOA News* on July 31, 2018 regarding President Trump speaking at rally in Tampa, Florida.

T-Brain's Two-Cents: Maybe we just turn this all into a space opera comedy with an orange-tinged supreme leader as the guy who loses?

> **PRESS:** Yes, Sarah. Last night [July 31, 2018], at the Tampa rally, the President again pushed for creation of a Space Force as a new military branch. The Defense Department today missed the deadline to submit a report to Congress about how this Space Force is to be structured. And we're told that the White House has now twice rejected drafts because the Defense Department doesn't want a Space Force. It would rather create a Space Command under the existing military structure.
>
> In view of this, how is the President going to force the creation of a Space Force?

SANDERS: We're continuing to work with the Department of Defense to figure out and determine the best way forward — something the President feels strongly about. And we're going to work with our team there and figure out the best solution.

– Press Secretary Sarah Sanders in James S. Brady Press Briefing Room beginning at 1:32 PM EDT on August 1, 2018 (Whitehouse.gov).

"NASA, which is making a BIG comeback under the Trump Administration, has just named 9 astronauts for Boeing and Spacex space flights. We have the greatest facilities in the world and we are now letting the private sector pay to use them. Exciting things happening. Space Force!"

(@realDonaldTrump)
Aug. 3, 2018, 3:43 PM. Tweet

"I'm hereby directing the Department of Defense and Pentagon to immediately begin the process necessary to establish a space force as the sixth branch of the armed forces."

– Trump in a statement released by the White House on August 9, 2018 (Whitehouse.gov).

T-Brain's Two-Cents: That's so adorable! You're such a kid at heart. (Wait…and of mind, too! Now that's not adorable. That's **very sad.**)

Space Force all the way!

(@realDonaldTrump)
Aug. 9, 2018, 9:03 AM. Tweet

"Since day one of our administration, @POTUS has kept his promise to restore America's proud legacy of leadership in space. Now the time has come to write the next great chapter in the history of our Armed Forces. The time has come to establish the United States #SpaceForce."

(@VP)
Aug. 10, 2018, 4:19 AM. Tweet

".@POTUS: "Just like the air, the land, the sea – space has become a warfighting domain. It is not enough to merely have an American presence in space – we must have American dominance in space." The time has come to establish the United States #SpaceForce."

(@VP)
Aug. 13, 2018, 1:53 PM. Tweet

There was opposition from Senators in both parties due to the cost and the potential increase in bureaucracy related to this Space Force idea. Sen. Dan Sullivan (R-AK), a members of the Senate Armed Services Committee, also commented that they should be focusing instead on the readiness level of the U.S.'s existing five services first since their readiness levels have dropped.

- This matter was mentioned in several articles, including one by *The Hill* that was dated August 21, 2018.

T-Brain's Two-Cents: Wait, **Trumpy**... Wasn't the Senate supposed to be on your side? Oopsie. Here's a *The Hill* article on that:

thehill.com/policy/defense/402748-senate-emerges-as-obstacle-to-trumps-space-force

"The #SpaceForce is an idea whose time has come. Just as our Nation established the Air Force to ensure American dominance in the skies in the mid-20th Century, in this still-new Century, we will create an armed service devoted solely to advancing American security in space."

(@VP)
Aug. 23, 2018, 11:32 AM. Tweet

T-Brain's Two-Cents: Surprise, surprise? Not really. He is after all…
Mr. One-Fast-Food-Bad-Heartburn-Away-From-Presidency?

A Simpleton Mind Threatened By… Sticks And Stones?

T-Brain's Two-Cents: President **Steel Courage**, do we need to keep at it with immigrant caravans? (I guess so until midterm elections end.)

PRESS: With the military, do you envision them firing upon any of these people?

PRESIDENT: I hope not.

PRESS: Could you see the military (inaudible)?

PRESIDENT: I hope not. It's the military — I hope — I hope there won't be that. But I will tell you this: Anybody throwing stones, rocks — like they did to Mexico and the Mexican military, Mexican police, where they badly hurt police and soldiers of Mexico — we will consider that a firearm. Because there's not much difference, where you get hit in the face with a rock — which, as you know, it was very violent a few days ago — very, very violent — that break-in. It was a break-in of a country. They broke into Mexico.

– Trump in the Roosevelt Room at the White House beginning at 4:19 PM EDT on November 1, 2018 (Whitehouse.gov).

Clueless Mind Of The First Ever… Worldwide Laughingstock?

T-Brain's Two-Cents: Wow, **Trumpmunch**! You sure did… **Make Laughingstocks Great Again!** They laughed right at you, no? Oops. Hey, check out these articles by *The Hill* dated September 2018:

thehill.com/homenews/administration/408260-un-audience-laughs-when-trump-boasts-of-achievements

thehill.com/homenews/administration/408642-trump-on-laughter-during-un-speech-they-werent-laughing-at-me-they

thehill.com/homenews/administration/408486-nikki-haley-claims-uns-laughter-at-trump-speech-showed-respect

PRESIDENT: Madam President, Mr. Secretary-General, world leaders, ambassadors, and distinguished delegates:

One year ago, I stood before you for the first time in this grand hall. I addressed the threats facing our world, and I presented a vision to achieve a brighter future for all of humanity. Today, I stand before the United Nations General Assembly to share the extraordinary progress we've made. In less than two years, my administration has accomplished more than almost any administration in the history of our country. America's — so true. (Laughter.)

Didn't expect that reaction, but that's okay. (Laughter and applause.)

– Trump at the United Nations Headquarters in New York, New York on September 25, 2018 (Whitehouse.gov).

T-Brain's Two-Cents: To those that don't like to read (Trumpistas?)… Just watch the video of **Trumpy's** U.N. 'speech.' And 2 ways to find the video that shows this beauty of his 'presidency.'

1) Search online by **googling** under the 'video' format search tab in a single search using these following words altogether as is:

united nations laughing president trump

2) Check out this link for a video by *VOA News*. The **30-second** incident begins at **1:02** out of this **36 minute, 33 second clip**:

www.youtube.com/watch?v=6pt-Dynpp6g

Unhinged Mind Of A Presidential Puppet?

"As my administration has demonstrated, America will always act in our national interest. I spoke before this body last year and warned that the U.N. Human Rights Council had become a grave embarrassment to this institution, shielding egregious human rights abusers while bashing America and its many friends. Our Ambassador to the United Nations, Nikki Haley, laid out a clear agenda for reform, but despite reported and repeated warnings, no action at all was taken.

"So the United States took the only responsible course: We withdrew from the Human Rights Council, and we will not return until real reform is enacted. For similar reasons, the United States will provide no support in recognition to the International Criminal Court. As far as America is concerned, the ICC has no jurisdiction, no legitimacy, and no authority. The ICC claims near-universal jurisdiction over the citizens of every country, violating all principles of justice, fairness, and due process. We will never surrender America's sovereignty to an unelected, unaccountable, global bureaucracy.

"America is governed by Americans. We reject the ideology of globalism, and we embrace the doctrine of patriotism."

– Trump speaks beginning at 10:38 AM EDT on September 25, 2018 at United Nations Headquarters in New York, New York (Whitehouse.gov).

T-Brain's Two-Cents: I struggled with how best to mock you on this one, but I decided to just let you **mock yourself** since you're simply so out of touch, you **bigly douche**.

An Atrophied Mind That Is Endangered By Its 'Tell'?

PRESS: Mr. President, what do you say to all the criticism of Matt Whitaker and the calls for him to recuse himself, given what he said about the Russian (inaudible)?

PRESIDENT: Well, Matt Whitaker — I don't know Matt Whitaker. Matt Whitaker worked for Jeff Sessions, and he was always extremely highly thought of, and he still is. But I didn't know Matt Whitaker. He worked for Attorney General Sessions. He was very, very highly thought of, and still is highly thought of. But this only comes up because anybody that works for me, they do a number on them.

But Matt Whitaker is a very smart man. He is a very respected man in the law enforcement community. Very respected; at the top of the line. And actually, the choice was greeted with raves, initially, and it still is in some circles. You know, it's a shame that no matter who I put in, they go after them. It's very sad, I have to say. But he's Acting. I think he'll do a very good job. And we'll see what happens.

But I will say this: Matt Whitaker is a very highly respected man, and you didn't have any problems with Matt Whitaker when he worked for Jeff Sessions. He's respected by law enforcement. He's a very strong law enforcement personality and person.

PRESS: Mr. President, did you talk with Matt Whitaker at all about the Mueller probe before you appointed him?

PRESIDENT: I didn't speak to Matt Whitaker about it. I don't know Matt Whitaker. Matt Whitaker has a great reputation, and that's what I wanted. I also wanted to do something which, frankly, I could have brought somebody very easily from the outside. I didn't want to do that. When Sessions left, what I did, very simply, is take a man who worked for Sessions. Again, he worked for Jeff Sessions. He's a highly respected man, especially by law enforcement. And I think he's going to do a great job. He's there in an acting position. He's a — probably, from what I hear — a very strong person, a very strong personality. And I think that's what they need.

PRESS: Is Kellyanne's husband's wrong?

PRESIDENT: Who?

PRESS: Kellyanne's husband wrote that the appointment was unconstitutional.

PRESIDENT: You mean Mr. Kellyanne Conway?

PRESS: He wrote that you're unconstitutionally appointing him. He is wrong?

PRESIDENT: He's just trying to get publicity for himself. Why don't you do this: Why don't you ask Kellyanne that question, all right? She might know him better than me. I really don't know the guy.

…

PRESS: On the Attorney General, what's your timeline to make a decision? And who are the frontrunners?

PRESIDENT: Well, I have some very, very good people. But, I mean, there's no rush. You know, it has to go through a Senate process, which takes a long time. But we'll pick somebody that's great. We're going to pick somebody that's very good. And again, I think it's very — Matt Whitaker is a highly respected man, but I didn't know Matt Whitaker. But he's a highly respected man.

PRESS: Mr. President, you said the Senate process. Matt Whitaker has not gone through a Senate process.

PRESIDENT: Yeah, but neither has Mueller.

…

PRESS: Do you expect Matt Whitaker to be involved in the Russia probe? Do you want him to —

PRESIDENT: It's up to him.

PRESS: Do you want him to rein in Robert Mueller?

PRESIDENT: What a stupid question that is. What a stupid question. But I watch you a lot. You ask a lot of stupid questions.

– Trump on the South Lawn beginning at 9:05 AM EST on November 9, 2018 (Whitehouse.gov).

T-Brain's Two-Cents: Stupid?! Well, even Forrest Gump is smarter and more accomplished than **Trumpy**. And he still has his hair, too.

"U.S. President Donald Trump seemed to distance himself on Friday [November 9, 2018] from his newly appointed acting attorney general Matt Whitaker, saying he doesn't 'know' the 49-year-old former U.S. attorney. ... William Gustoff, who co-founded a law firm with Whitaker in 2009 and remains friendly with him, said Trump's comment may simply mean that the president doesn't 'really know him,' not that the two are not acquainted with each other.

"Other friends and associates of Whitaker said the former Iowa college football star has forged a close working relationship with Trump since his appointment last fall as chief of staff to then-attorney general Jeff Sessions. The relationship developed as Whitaker began accompanying Sessions to White House meetings after joining the Justice Department from the Foundation for Accountability and Civic Trust (FACT), a conservative ethics monitoring group that has filed complaints against Democratic politicians. ...

"Trump's assertion that he doesn't know Whitaker directly contradicts what he told Fox News last month [October 11, 2018], when he said, 'I mean, I know Matt Whitaker' and that he is 'a great guy.' CNN also reported that Whitaker has visited the White House a dozen or more times since becoming Sessions' chief of staff and that he had a good relationship with the president."

– Reported by *VOA News* on November 10, 2018 in regards to Trump's comments about Matt Whitaker that Trump made on November 9, 2018 and October 11, 2018.

T-Brain's Two-Cents: Alright, I mean, **I know Trumpy** since after all I'm his damned brain. He's sort of a great guy but maybe **a liddle' slow on the uptake**... actually, like really *really* freakin' slow and... sometimes a bit off with understanding, I think, everything. **Everything**.

F. Genuinely Extremely Thoughtful?

A 'Hard-To-Believe-But-We-*Think*-We-Found-*ONE*' Moment?

PRESS: Mr. President, are you thinking about more Supreme Court justices since Justice Ginsburg in the hospital?

PRESIDENT: No, I wish her well. She said something very inappropriate during the campaign, but she apologized for it. I wouldn't say she's exactly on my side, but I wish her well. I hope she gets better. And I hope she serves on the Supreme Court for many, many years.

– Trump on the South Lawn beginning at 9:05 AM EST on November 9, 2018 (Whitehouse.gov).

T-Brain's Two-Cents: Well, I had to try to end this Mockiography™ branded satirical novel in a positive note. So it's nice to see here that **Trumpy** is somewhat human… unless, of course, it's just a glitch… in the matrix.

Why Can't We Just Let Friends Be Friends, No?

<u>*T-Brain's Two-Cents:*</u> Hey, even I told **Trumpy** that this photo op might just not look too good for him and he shrugged and responded to me, **T-Brain**, with a certain slight accent… 'Forget about it!'

HIGHLIGHTS, INDEX & GLOSSARY
(AKA "HIGHDEXLOSSARY")

President Trump said he has great confidence in his own,   96
Intelligence community (or agencies),   21-2, 55, 96
    President Trump says that he has 'full faith and support' for
        America's great,   22
    According to the press, the conclusion that Russia interfered in
        the 2016 elections was reached by the American,   96
Intelligence Quotient (I.Q.),   128, 143
    President Trump remarks that he has one of the highest,   128
Intelligent,   89
    very,   89
ISIS,   15
Ivy League school (or college),   89, 129, 183
    was a "nice student" when I went to an,   89
    I attended the best colleges but only one of which was an,   129
    but it appears that President Trump attended only for 24 months
        (or more likely than not just roughly *18 months* of actual
            studying at) an,   187
    in contrast, one of the *Verbatimly, Trump* authors attended (in
        their first try and) for *all 4 years* at 1 college that was an, 183

J
#JobsNotMobs,   51

K
#KnobsNotMobs,   51
K-Con,   120
    with mixed emotions, T-Brain refers to Kellyanne Conway, in
        shorthand, as,   120
Kelly, John F.,   49
Kennedy, John F.,   134
Kilmeade, Brian,   115

L
Lack, Andy,   142
Lee, Mike,   vii
Love, Mia,   145

M
#ManUp   109, 123, 125
McBrain,   vii
    brain of Mitch McConnell is nicknamed by the authors as,   vii

IMAGE CREDITS

Disclaimer: No endorsements were given by any of the original authors of the images shown herein for their images' inclusion in this novel, for any modifications to the original images or for any of the captions/descriptions that were placed alongside the images.

Image of silhouette on the page titled "**WANTED**" (p. iii): Courtesy of "SVG SILH" (CC0 1.0). Links to the original image and its license:

//svgsilh.com/image/2789735.html
//creativecommons.org/publicdomain/zero/1.0/

Image of brain(s) and original descriptors shown on cover and/or on the page titled "**HIGHER THAN A+**" (p. iv): Courtesy of OpenStax Copyright Holders (Rice University Publishers: OpenStax Biology) (CC BY 3.0). Image shown herein was modified from the original image. Links to the original image and its license:

//commons.wikimedia.org/wiki/File:Figure_35_03_05_Brain_size_Vertical.png
//creativecommons.org/licenses/by/3.0/deed.en

Image of "poop" that is labeled as "F." on the page titled "**HIGHER THAN A+**" (p. iv): Courtesy of "Clker-Free-Vector-Images / 29588 images". Image shown herein modified from the original image. Links to the original image and its license:

//pixabay.com/vectors/poop-bowel-movement-crap-stink-311256/
//pixabay.com/service/license/

Image of "A+" that is at the top of the page titled "**HIGHER THAN A+**" (p. iv): Courtesy of Olivia Jester, "School 2," (CC0 1.0). Image shown herein was modified from the original image. Links to the original image and its license:

//www.publicdomainpictures.net/en/view-image.php?image=184564&picture=school-2
//creativecommons.org/publicdomain/zero/1.0/

Image titled "**Mr. High-IQ… Now As A Bully In His Prime?**" (p. ix): Courtesy of Wikimedia Commons contributors (18 December 2017); Ali Shaker/VOA, "Republican presidential nominee Donald Trump, left, gives his running mate, Indiana Governor Mike Pence, a thumbs up after Pence addressed the Republican National Convention," 20 July 2016. Image shown herein was modified from the original image and its original size. Links to images and its terms:

//commons.wikimedia.org/wiki/File:Donald_Trump_RNC_July_2016_(1).jpg

Original source:
//www.voanews.com/usa/live-blog-republican-national-convention-day-3
//www.voanews.com/terms-use-and-privacy-notice

Image titled "**Adorable-Baby-In-Chief**" (p. xi): Courtesy of Michael Reeve, "Trump Awakens: The Trump Baby blimp rises over London's Parliament Square," 13 July 2018 (CC BY-SA 2.0). Image shown herein was modified from the original image. Links to the original image and its license:

//www.flickr.com/photos/mykreeve/43381966091
//creativecommons.org/licenses/by-sa/2.0/

Image titled "**Best-Jobs-President-Of-All-Mankind**" (p. xi): Courtesy of Ross Sneddon, "Edinburgh, United Kingdom: A team of 'Trump babysitters' hold on to the giant balloon of Donald Trump, with thousands of on-lookers," 29 July 2018, on Unsplash.com. Image shown herein was modified. Links to the original image and its license:

//unsplash.com/photos/bDDZfkWGl4Y
//unsplash.com/@rosssneddon
//unsplash.com/license

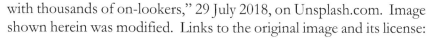

Image titled **"Why Can't We Just Let Friends Be Friends, No?"** (p. 166): Courtesy of The White House, "President Donald J. Trump and President Vladimir Putin of the Russian Federation," 16 July 2018 (CC Public Domain Mark 1.0) (Official White House Photo by Shealah Craighead). Links to the original image and its license:

//www.flickr.com/photos/whitehouse/42547210635
//creativecommons.org/publicdomain/mark/1.0/

DEDICATIONS 2.0
(Sorry, but on a serious note…)

This book is dedicated to United States military veterans. Without their sacrifices America would never have been able to shine for all as a beacon of freedom and opportunity unlike anywhere else in this imperfect world. And despite our own imperfections there is still no other nation that has shed more of its own blood for the aid, protection and freedom of others far beyond its borders.

So a heartfelt thanks to all who have served for the United States of America – including my friends, family members and so many others; and especially to the late former U.S. Senator John S. McCain, III as well as the late President George H.W. Bush – both of whom indisputably deserved nothing short of absolute respect, admiration and gratitude.

Messrs. McCain and Bush, two of America's last great soldier-statesmen, lived their lives exuding humility and self-sacrifice, exhibited courage when choosing to not take routes of ease and convenience, and taught us all that selfless public service is most noble and unquestionably necessary.

– Anonymous – Co-author of *Verbatimly, Trump*

Above all else, this book is dedicated to my own family who inspire me and to my parents and paternal grandfather who asked for so little yet deserved so much.

Without their own sacrifices I would have never been given the incredible opportunity in this remarkable land to achieve whatever I envisioned and desired – while many others elsewhere sadly can only dream of such things.

– Meyer VII, Cam S. – Co-author of *Verbatimly, Trump*